MEMORY ETERNAL

Living with Grief
as Orthodox Christians

SARAH BYRNE-MARTELLI

ANCIENT FAITH PUBLISHING

CHESTERTON, INDIANA

Published by:
  Ancient Faith Publishing
  A Division of Ancient Faith Ministries
  P.O. Box 748
  Chesterton, IN 46304

Unless otherwise noted, Scripture quotations are taken from the New
King James Version, © 1979, 1980, 1982 by Thomas Nelson, Inc. Used by
permission.

ISBN: 978-1-955890-18-2

Library of Congress Control Number: 2022937554

*This book is dedicated to my parents, Nancy and Bill Byrne.
Thank you for everything. —SBM*

Contents

Foreword

ORTHODOX CHRISTIANS UNDERSTAND grief differently from non-Christians and even non-Orthodox. For Orthodox Christians, death is understood as the last enemy. We were created by God to enjoy His love, know Him, and be known by Him. Adam's choice to be without God broke the natural order revealed to us by God. This choice resulted in a different life, which included difficulty communing with God and each other, and finally resulted in death. This life journey is a gift to bring us home to God, though this journey includes struggles, suffering, and death. God did not leave us outside of His love but gave us a plan for redemption through Christ.

After destroying death by dying, Christ established for us the Church. This Church is a gift from God to guide us through life and into Christ and His eternity. It is through the Church that we are grafted to God in baptism. It is through the Church that we are fed by God in the Eucharist. It is in the Church that we encounter God through real Christian fellowship and caring. It is in the Church that we are given the tools to understand our meaning and discover our vocations. It is in the Church that we become Christians and ourselves reclaim His world to make it holy.

Bodily sickness and death are now (since the Fall) part of our redemptive journeys. While sickness is often a temptation to leave God and be filled with grieving for ourselves, members of our natural and church families can strengthen us and keep us focused on Christ. When we ourselves grieve the losses of our loved ones, again our families can remind us of God's presence with us and His love for us. We who are in the Church are called to witness to each other. This is the real meaning of Christian fellowship. Such fellowship is more than cooking at church fundraisers or bowling with the parish league. Christian fellowship is bearing one another's burdens and witnessing to God's redemptive love. It is through each other that we encounter God in our homes, hospitals, and even funeral parlors.

Grieving is the only healthy response to death. To lose a partner, parent, child, or friend and not care would indeed be unhealthy. We observe that all human beings, and for that matter some animals, grieve the loss of companions. Grieving is a personal experience as well as a communal experience within the Church. The church community teaches us how to grieve, in St. Paul's words, in the hope of the Resurrection. It allows us to connect with one another even when we feel alone in a crowd. This is because other believers share in the same hope, a hope that defines us as Christians. We are, above all other descriptors, the people of the Resurrected One. We are the people who know the tomb of Christ is empty; God and eternity are at hand.

When Christ died on the Cross, the earth trembled, and the curtain of the temple was rent in two (Matt. 27:22). The dead are not far away but in Christ. The curtain symbolizes the separation created by sin as well as the gates of Hades that once held us captive. By dying, Christ who is life itself joins us to His eternal life. In His bodily Resurrection, we too are bodily resurrected. This is because we were joined to Him in baptism.

Together in Christ, we remember each other and can grow to recognize our oneness again. To *re-member* means to put back together again. We call each other to mind in order to realize that we are together in Christ once more. At first, remembering can be painful, but in time, if we embrace this pain, we can use it to become one with our loved ones once more.

In this book, Chaplain Sarah Byrne-Martelli offers insights from her research about grieving Orthodox Christians along with a review of Orthodox theology and bereavement theory. She analyzes how Orthodox people process grief and loss through the lens of faith and provides a bereavement curriculum for use in parishes or small groups. She has discovered a treasure of information that will normalize our experiences and offer us ways to function better, get along better with others, and draw on the wisdom of our Holy Tradition. This book offers parish priests and other church leaders information that will allow local parishes to better meet the needs of their grieving members. Through a mix of meaningful stories and theological and liturgical reflections, Sarah gives us tools to better minister to each other, both in groups and in person-to-person encounters. I thank Sarah for her good work, and I commend it.

+JOHN, Bishop of Worcester and New England
Antiochian Orthodox Christian Archdiocese
of New York and North America

Introduction

DURING A SUMMER of deep grief, I embarked on a week-long retreat at an Orthodox Christian monastery. I offered myself time to rest, to read, and to pray. On a hot morning in July, I started on an ambitious hike through the forest on the monastery grounds. The trees and greenery were abuzz in that perfect midsummer way. It was clear that no one had walked that path in days.

Spiderwebs glistened with dew, connecting tree to tree, and the birds chirped antiphonally from their perches. I walked along steadily, swatting the flies circling my head. Everything was green, vibrant, lively. All of creation seemed to be rejoicing, and yet I felt nothing but empty and lost. I felt as if I were wearing a blanket made of cement. I was glad the forest had only one path so I didn't have to choose which way to go.

I crested the top of a small hill and started to hike down. Suddenly I hit a patch of wet moss on a flat rock, and my feet slipped out from underneath me. My body hit the ground. I zoomed down this natural slide and landed in a muddy, sweaty, undignified heap at the bottom. I whimpered, and then the laughing began. I laughed and laughed until I cried. I cried because I'd fallen; I cried because the life I had known had ended; I cried because everything was in flux and unclear and broken.

Slowly, out of movement came stillness as I sat there on the ground. And then out of the cacophony of the forest came a loving presence: the *kol d'mama dakah*, the still, small voice of God. It occurred to me that the only thing that does not change— amidst our losses, our questions, our brokenness and fumbling and falling—is God. God is the ground below us, the "ground of being" as Paul Tillich has called Him, the One who enlivens us all. I was humbled, and God was there to receive me.

The word *humility* comes from the Latin word *humus*, which means "fertile ground." Metropolitan Anthony Bloom has written, "Humility is the situation of the earth."[1] He reminds us how the earth holds us, "silent and accepting everything and in a miraculous way making out of all the refuse new richness . . . open to the sunshine, open to the rain, ready to receive any seed we sow."[2] So it is with grief. It humbles us, sometimes even into a pathetic, muddy, half-laughing, half-crying heap on the ground. In being humbled, we are forced to listen and be still and know that God is God.

Presumably, you are reading this book because you are grieving, or because you love someone who is grieving, or because you want to learn more about grief. I welcome you just as you are. The grief of losing a loved one is universal and yet often feels personal, unique, and isolating. You may feel as if you are going crazy, or you will never stop crying, or you will never start crying because you are too numb. You may forget what you're doing while you're doing it. You may feel as if you're carrying a wet blanket all the time or your heart has been replaced by a heavy stone. You may wake up and enjoy three seconds of peace before the weight and memory of your loss come crashing down on you. You remember. You always remember.

You may think any or all of these things:

» *I have no one who understands.*
» *People have stopped talking to me about my loved one.*
» *I feel isolated.*
» *People don't know what to say.*
» *They say "she's in a better place," but I know a better place would be with me.*
» *People are avoiding me.*
» *No one says my loved one's name anymore.*
» *I feel as if I have to be done with my grief right away.*
» *I don't know how to deal with these feelings.*
» *I want people to stop telling me my loved one is a new angel in heaven.*
» *My spouse and I are grieving differently, and I can't deal with it.*
» *I feel as if God has abandoned me.*
» *The holidays are too hard for me.*

When people ask you how you are, they tilt their head in a way that implies they know you might cry when they ask. You debate whether you should say, "Oh, you know, I'm hanging in there!" or perhaps, "Frankly I'm losing it. I want to curl up in a ball and I'm angry all the time." You tend to give the first response, but here and there you let others know how you really are.

My prayer is that, amidst all this, you will allow yourself to be held by God. God is the ground of our being and the Being who holds us and loves us—steady, unchanging, sturdy. May you be humbled and held. May your healing begin even when you feel you are falling. May you know in your deepest heart that God is with you in your grief.

In a way, this book started writing itself during my adolescence. When I was a teenager, my thirteen-year-old cousin Joey died in a tragic skiing accident. I grew up in a large, loud, close-knit family in upstate New York: Irish Catholic on my dad's side of the family, Presbyterian on my mom's side, with Jewish and evangelical cousins. I remember seeing so many of my cousins, aunts, and uncles at Joey's wake and funeral. I remember how they played the Led Zeppelin song "Stairway to Heaven," his favorite. I remember hugging Joey's parents in the receiving line as they wept.

I remember seeing Joey's body at his wake. He looked peaceful. I was surprised to see one of my Catholic aunts lean down and kiss him in his casket. She did this lovingly and naturally. As I was raised Presbyterian, I was not used to attending wakes, or seeing open caskets, or touching those who had died. This image of my aunt bestowing one last kiss on Joey's head is as clear to me today as it was so many years ago, and just as powerful. May Joey's memory be eternal.

Shortly afterward, I suffered the tragic loss of a dear and beautiful friend, Flavia, from my high school gymnastics team. She died in a car accident, a victim of the icy roads of upstate New York winters. I recall sitting in a classroom with my beloved teammates, crying and talking and supporting one another. I remember hugging a close friend in the high school hallway, holding on for dear life; I still vividly recall the physical sensation of crying onto his ivory-colored wool fisherman's sweater. We experience grief in our bodies. May Flavia's memory be eternal.

The next year, I lost another gymnastics teammate, Nancy, who died by suicide. Nancy had the sweetest, silliest temperament, with huge dimples to match. She had just started her freshman year in college while I was a senior in high school. We were committed pen-pals that year; she sent me hilarious hand-drawn cartoons and doodles, the envelopes adorned with rainbow stickers and balloon lettering. I remember the moment when, as I stood in the kitchen with my family, the nightly news reported that Nancy had died. I felt my breath leave my body; I became instantly numb, and I didn't know whether to cry, scream, or collapse to the floor.

At her funeral, our gymnastics team gathered yet again to mourn the death of one of our own. I'd had no idea how much Nancy was struggling. No one did. I will never know what agony her heart was carrying or what pain was hidden deep within her. Our hugs, our tears, and our prayers expressed the questions that no one could answer. May Nancy's memory be eternal.

As a young person, I was allowed to grieve. I was given time to cry, space to talk and process my sadness, people to hug, and a chance to attend the funerals. I am eternally grateful that my teenage grief was not shoved under the rug or minimized in any way. I learned how to grieve in my community, both formally in church and informally with friends and family who loved me.

These losses and others have led me to where and who I am today: an Orthodox Christian, a wife and mother, a board-certified health care chaplain, and a bereavement counselor. I was received into the Orthodox Church in 2002, though I do not exactly think of myself as a convert. Joining the Church felt like a natural continuation of the support and faith of my parents, the love of my Presbyterian Church community, the experiences of bar mitzvahs and first communions with my Jewish and Catholic cousins, my summers dancing as a child at St. Sophia's Greek Fest, and much more. (Truthfully, it was probably the *loukoumades* at St. Sophia's that clinched the deal!)

I was a religion major in college and studied abroad in Athens, Greece. The first Orthodox Christian service I attended was vespers at the Monastery of the Annunciation in Ormylia, Halkidiki. A hundred nuns chanted the most glorious hymnody I had ever heard. That was it: my steady path into the Orthodox Church had begun. God called me into this life and this vocation, and for this I am grateful.

Many people ask me how I can bear to do the work of health care chaplaincy, with so much death, tragedy, and grief. I bear it through my life in the Church: the sacraments, the fellowship, the prayers. I bear it by moving through it, trying to use my gifts, praying for the people I care for, and letting myself cry when I need to cry. I have cared for hundreds of people at the end of life, and I have supported grieving people in their darkest days.

I would never be able to do this work with my own skills alone. The only way I can do it is by constantly (and imperfectly) offering my prayers and my work to God: God who is love and light and healing. Not me, but Christ in me: Lord, I believe; help my unbelief! The way we bear the grief of this world is through what we have already been given in the life of the Church.

Our Church has a wealth of resources that teach us how to mourn, comfort us, and show us how to live in the wake of a loss. Our faith practices—including our sacraments, liturgical gestures, texts, and traditions—teach us how to grieve. We profess that Christ has trampled down death by death, and on those who are in the tombs, He has bestowed life. Those who have died are yet alive in Christ. We proclaim a faith that lifts up the cross of Christ with both sorrow and joy, and we find rest and peace in God's love for all His people.

Our theological tradition and our liturgical practices reveal to us a life that finds its meaning and shape in the Person of Christ. This includes the way Christ was born, lived, cared for others, grieved, died, and rose from the dead. The experience of grief calls us to deepen our willingness to trust God: "For if we live, we live to the Lord; and if we die, we die to the Lord. Therefore, whether we live or die, we are the Lord's. For to this end Christ died, and rose and lived again, that he might be Lord of both the dead and the living" (Rom. 14:8, 9). The life of faith teaches us how to experience grief with the support of our neighbors in the Body of Christ.

The Reverend Frederick Buechner has said, "The place God calls you to is the place where your deep gladness and the world's deep hunger meet." We are called, as members of the Church, to continuously discern the "world's deep hunger." My "deep gladness" comes not merely from a place of professional expertise as a chaplain or from my personal family or faith, though that is part of it. Instead, my gladness emerges from the astonishingly rich and wide tradition of compassion and hope within our faith. My gladness comes from knowing that God is with us in life and in death. The more grieving people I meet and the more faith I witness, the stronger my own faith grows. I pray this gladness will reach you and all those whose hearts are in pain after facing the death of a loved one.

During my doctoral studies at St. Vladimir's Orthodox Theological Seminary, I conducted qualitative research with Orthodox Christians who were grieving. My research revealed many themes that are found in secular bereavement literature, such as isolation, identity loss, and disconnection. I explored the unique ways in which Orthodox people conceptualize grief differently from non-Orthodox people. My hope is that the stories and reflections from wonderful interviewees included in this book will resonate with you and reassure you that you don't have to grieve alone.

There is something particular about our tradition that helps us, or should help us, to grieve differently from others and perhaps in a healthier way. The concept of "memory eternal," the way we hold memorials, our understanding of joyful sorrow, the cross and resurrection, the presence and veneration of the body at the funeral, and the centrality of praying for the dead are key ways we grieve. There are rich tensions at play in our funeral hymnography; for example, we emphasize the sadness of loss while recalling the peace granted to those who fall asleep in the Lord.

We can fully reject the popular idea that we have to "get over" a death, or that after one year, our time of grief is neatly finished. Instead, we find a new way to relocate our loved ones in our hearts within the greater context of the living faith community. I found that many of us stay connected to loved ones—even those with whom we have had a complicated relationship—and are comforted by this connection, even after death.

This book has three sections. In Section I, "Death, Grief, and the Life of the Church," I explore what Scripture, liturgy, and theology teach us about death, the cross, and grief. This is the framework that helps us understand our grief. Allow yourself time to look through the funeral texts, the Scripture readings, and the prayers. They are so rich and meaningful. It would probably take a lifetime to explore it all, but we will do our best.

In Section II, "Living and Grieving as Orthodox Christians," we dive into the stories of real Orthodox people who have coped with many types of grief. Their stories are profound, raw, honest, and inspiring. I hope they will provoke reflection and resonate with you. In this section, I also address several key themes of grief, including emotions, self-care, the role of community, continuing bonds, the value of parish life, and the meaning of grieving as an Orthodox Christian.

In Section III, "The Memory Eternal Bereavement Group Guide," I offer you an eight-part guide to processing grief with others. In this section, I offer prayers, quotes, grief activities, and reflection questions to help you explore your grief. Ideally, this guide will be used in a parish setting for a structured weekly bereavement group. It could also be used in an online group. If such a group is not yet available in your area, consider starting one! Such a group can be led by any willing Orthodox Christian. A facilitator's guide is provided in Appendix I. Please note: If the group format does not appeal to you, you can certainly go through the curriculum on your own, responding to the reflection questions in a journal. Or perhaps you could complete the curriculum with a trusted friend or family member. I thank you in advance for participating in or leading a bereavement group.

I hope this book will empower you to make use of the vast resources of our faith for processing grief. I hope it will connect you with others on a richer level than usual, with a bond of Christian community that goes deeper than the average conversation. The acts of living and dying and grieving as a Christian require engagement with the sacramental life of the Church in community, sharing our experiences and supporting each other. Our tradition has a rich, deep vision of what it means to die and live again with Christ. Simply, we should not grieve alone.

Never forget: God is always with us through life and death and every experience of joy and sorrow. As a grieving chaplain friend once said to me, "We are swimming in an ocean of God! Everything is from God. Everything."

Death, Grief, and the Life of the Church

CHAPTER ONE

Understanding Death through the Cross

How do orthodox Christians view death? Is it something to hold in hopeful prayer, as we pray in the Divine Liturgy for a "Christian ending to our lives, painless, blameless, and peaceful"? Is death something to be feared? Something to be mourned? A natural part of life that we should contemplate? As with many deep questions of faith and practice, there is no simple answer. Or perhaps the answer to all of these key questions is yes.

Death is an unavoidable part of our human existence. It is the one "fixed, inevitable event to which every human must look forward."[3] The traditional interpretation of the Genesis account teaches us that death is unnatural, contrary to God's original intention for us, and the result of sin (Gen. 3:17–19). Thus, in a sense, we must not embrace death as a natural or welcomed part of life. One of our great contemporary theologians, Fr. Alexander Schmemann, writes in *The Liturgy of Death* that death was "not created by God . . . it is not, in the emphatic sense of the word, a 'natural' event."[4] It is a tragedy on the deepest level, for God created us not that we should die but in order that we should live fully.

Death has also been characterized as an enemy. Saint Paul proclaims, "For He must reign till He has put all enemies under His feet. The last enemy that will be destroyed is death" (1 Cor. 15:25, 26). Though death is both a tragedy and an enemy, Christ's life-giving death is His gift to us, an expression of His mercy and compassion. It is a gift because through death, God creates us anew, uniting us in resurrection and recreating us in the fullness of life.

The priest and theologian Fr. John Behr has written extensively about death, the cross, and theological anthropology. He asserts that we cannot understand death until we contemplate Christ's death upon the cross. The transforming power of God is "demonstrated through the death of Christ: not simply his death, by being put to death, but by voluntary death, going to the Cross in obedience to the Father."[5] It is on the cross that Christ fulfills His nature, both divine and human. Christ's "taking upon himself the role of a servant" does not diminish our perception of His divinity but "actually manifests his true divinity."[6] Through the cross, we are given a vision of Jesus Christ as fully human and fully divine.

We understand Christ's death and resurrection through participating in the liturgical life of the community. "It is truly through the church," St. Gregory of Nyssa says in his Commentary on the Song of Songs, that we encounter "God's manifold wisdom, which marvelously works great wonders through opposites: how life came through death, righteousness through sin, blessing through curse, glory through disgrace, strength through weakness."[7] He notes, "It is not the human nature that raises up Lazarus, nor is it the power that cannot suffer that weeps for him when he lies in the grave; the tear is a property of the man, the life from the true Life."[8]

Father Behr writes, "The cross is properly said to be the Cross of the Lord of glory and Jesus is confessed as Lord to the glory of the Father."[9] It is precisely on the cross that death itself is transformed and Christ's glory is revealed. For St. Gregory, the "identity of the one Lord Christ hangs on the cross, known, no longer after the flesh, as one put to death, but in the Spirit, as one who gave himself to death, so conquering death."[10]

Father Behr reminds us that Christ's victory over death is not simply metaphorical; He "rose bodily from the dead to sit with the Father."[11] His victory enables us "to see a further aspect to the mystery of Christ in our actual bodily death: the sowing of the mortal body in the ground so that, dying, it may rise as a spiritual body."[12] Our life as members of Christ's body reaches fulfillment in death, and our death reaches fulfillment in Christ.

Our faith is fulfilled in the Person of Christ, fully human and fully God. In "The Word of the Cross," Fr. Thomas Hopko of blessed memory reminds us that the cross is the center of everything:

> The very center of our worship is "This is my Body, broken; this is my Blood, shed for the life of the world." It's our very center of everything, and that's why in the middle of Lent we put the cross out all week, that's why the whole year is centered around the passion of Christ and his victorious Resurrection, the Pascha of the Cross, as it says, the old saying in Greek: "*Pascha Stavrou* ēmon, *Pascha tēs [Anastaseōs]*—the Pascha of [our] Cross, the Pascha of the Resurrection."[13]

The cross is where God speaks to us and embodies His final and most powerful words. As Christ awaited His death, He said, "It is finished." As Fr. Hopko notes, "When Jesus, hanging on the Cross, says, 'It is fulfilled'—*tetelestai*, sometimes translated, 'It is finished,' it doesn't simply mean it's the end of the story. It means that it's the total accomplishment of everything. Everything now is done."[14] Every ounce of suffering, every fear, every pain, every bit of brokenness is made whole. God has accomplished everything, and death is overthrown.

We sing of salvation on the Feast of the Cross; the Psalms proclaim, "God has worked salvation in the midst of the earth" (Ps. 73:12). The salvation we proclaim comes to fulfillment when Christ is "lifted upon the Cross, when he is crucified. That's the ultimate, definitive, absolute, total, perfect, unsurpassable act, word, revelation, manifestation of God."[15] What else can we say?

Ultimately, the cross teaches us how to be silent—silent in death, silent in contemplation, silent in humility. In the "silent depth of the Cross, the silence of God, which is more eloquent than any word, speaks to *our* silence, the silence within us, in order that we can then understand and grasp and live the deepest mysteries of God."[16] In this silence, we learn how to grieve, and we follow the example of Christ Himself.

CHAPTER TWO

Grief and Lamentation

THE SCRIPTURES OFFER us many examples of grief and
lamentation. In the Psalms, we see how King David
lamented: "My heart is severely pained within me, and the ter-
rors of death have fallen upon me. Fearfulness and trembling
have come upon me, and horror has overwhelmed me" (Ps. 55:4,
5). Psalm 6:3 cries out, "My soul also is greatly troubled; But
You, O Lord—how long?" We hear tearful prayers seeking the
Lord's comfort: "My soul thirsts for God, for the living God.
When shall I come and appear before God? My tears have been
my food day and night, while they continually say to me, 'Where
is your God?' When I remember these things, I pour out my soul
within me" (Ps. 42:2–4). The emotions of grief are unavoidable
in the face of loss, and we join a great cloud of witnesses when
we lament.

Jesus' actions demonstrated that death is a cause for grief
and lament. He expressed profound sadness alongside Martha
and Mary of Bethany as He wept for his friend Lazarus. Those
who were near Jesus on that day interpreted His weeping as
loving grief: "See how He loved him!" (John 11:36). However,

Jesus' weeping at Lazarus's grave is not merely emotional. Leading up to this event, Christ had been teaching about the resurrection. Hence His response carries with it a unique "grief over the lack of faith of several bystanders" and even grief "over the power that death, as the last enemy, still exercises."[17] Christ's grief is heightened within the greater context of His life and anticipated death and Resurrection.

At Christ's death, His friends and followers experienced profound grief. They lamented because He was removed from His people: "But the days will come when the bridegroom will be taken away from them, and then they will fast in those days" (Mark 2:20). His separation from His people brought them grief and confusion. Christ's followers, and notably His mother, Mary, stood vigil at the cross as He died (John 19:25). One can only imagine their sadness and confusion as they witnessed His crucifixion.

After Christ's burial, Mary Magdalene stood by the tomb weeping, and "as she wept she stooped down and looked into the tomb. And she saw two angels in white sitting, one at the head and the other at the feet, where the body of Jesus had lain. Then they said to her, 'Woman, why are you weeping?'" (John 20:11–13). Jesus then revealed Himself to her. She was tasked with sharing the good news of His Resurrection with the world.

We see expressions of grief in Scripture on the death of the first Christian martyr: "Devout men carried Stephen to his burial, and made great lamentation over him" (Acts 8:2). We see this at the death of Tabitha: "All the widows stood by him (Peter) weeping" (Acts 9:39). Those who carried the hope of eternal life were not expected to hide their sorrow over the loss of loved ones.

Again, our tradition teaches us that grief responses are understandable and that lamentation is part of life. Only by contemplating death fully and with open and lamenting hearts may we come to understand that Christ's death is our liberation, "upon those in the tombs bestowing life!"

Grieving with Hope

Saint Paul teaches us that we are not to grieve "as others who have no hope" (1 Thess. 4:23). What does it mean to grieve with hope? Does it mean to put on a brave face, even amid sorrow? These questions have been the subject of much theological reflection; some scholars have encouraged a distinction between "grieving *per se*, which would be acceptable, and grieving excessively, as if completely bereft of hope, which would be characteristic of the grieving of pagans."[18] How should the gospel of resurrection shape our grief response? Is it just a matter of really believing in the resurrection and therein finding comfort? Or is there a way to honor the fact that we are incarnate and emotional beings who are able to hope and lament at the same time?

Saint Gregory of Nyssa offers us this middle road, which takes into account the sorrow of death while teaching us how to grieve with hope. He experienced his own great losses: his brother St. Naucratius, his brother St. Basil, Bishop of Caesarea, and his sister St. Macrina. Saint Gregory's *On the Soul and Resurrection* offers us a dialogue at the dying Macrina's bedside wherein St. Gregory has an opportunity to process his grief for their newly deceased brother, St. Basil. Saint Macrina guides him through his sorrow: "She, like an expert equestrian, allowed me briefly to be carried away by the torrent of my grief."[19]

Saint Gregory's full treatise, written after St. Macrina's death, is beyond the scope of our discussion, but it is interesting to examine how he addresses his own grief after her death. Saint Gregory is "numbed with grief" over St. Macrina's death, and when he "hears the mournful wailing of the virgins of the community, St. Gregory comments, 'My reason no longer remained steady, but as if submerged by a torrent in flood, was swept under by passion. . . . I yielded myself up wholly to the lamentations.'"[20] Saint Gregory is gentle with the grief of others in St. Macrina's community: "The virgins' grief seemed just and commendable" because they lamented the loss of a great teacher.[21] He goes to great lengths to describe the depths of their grief expressions. He does not downplay their lamentations. He acknowledges that it is possible to sustain hope while lamenting loss.

Saint Gregory encourages grievers to "express their horrific pain"; importantly, his reason for allowing lamentation is his "anticipation that once their mourning has exhausted itself, they will be open to the hope that the gospel offers."[22] Ultimately, the soul's "reasoning faculty," which confesses Christ's resurrection, and "the passions of the soul are intimately related and mutually affect one another."[23] By expressing grief out loud, we actually allow the passions to be "depleted so that the message of hope can then be properly heard."[24]

Put simply, grief should not remain bottled up. We must move all the way through lamentation in order to arrive at a place where we are open to hope and restoration. Expressing grief leaves us renewed and cleansed; after we wipe away our tears, we may achieve a new level of hope.

Surviving the Pain of Grief

How do we survive in the face of grief and loss? We survive as did the myrrhbearers. We survive in prayer, and in community, and in faith. Those who anticipate the hope of eternal life are not expected to hide their sorrow over the loss of loved ones. We have faith in the ultimate goodness and triumphal love of God through Christ. We grieve as those who find meaning in Christ's gift of eternal life.

Father Schmemann exhorts us to rediscover death in a tripartite vision of tragedy, victory, and hope. He calls us to rediscover death as a tragedy: an "ontological catastrophe" worthy of genuine lament. He views death as a victory: the "victory over death achieved by Christ."[25] And finally, he challenges us to "rediscover death as hope: that mounting light described in the hymn to the Theotokos that speaks of the 'dawn of the mystical day.'"[26] This approach grants us the space to grieve, to cry, and to lament. It does not assign any limits to our grief but instead frames Christian grief through a hopeful lens of sorrowful joy, calling us always to honor our loved ones in our eternal memories.

We wait in prayerful anticipation to rise again with Christ. Death has been defeated through the cross and the resurrection on the third day. Those who fall asleep in the Lord are welcomed to a place of rest and peace. We are called to a balance of simultaneous joy and grief, cross and resurrection, fear and anticipation, separation and reunion. Christ is the one who heals, who consoles, and who co-suffers with us, even unto death.

CHAPTER THREE

Praying Through our Grief in Liturgy

O UR FAITH TEACHES us how to think about grief and death as well as how to act. It teaches us how to be present, both mentally and physically. We know how to practice liturgical vigil, standing at the cross of Holy Friday, keeping watch and praying the Psalms. We know how to stand in the dark and wait in prayerful hope as we anticipate the Paschal hymn, "Come receive the light." We know how to keep watch in prayer and in quiet anticipation. We have the spiritual endurance gained from many hours of prayer and worship. What a gift we are given! What a gift we may offer to our friends and loved ones. We may embody the best way to be brave and to be present, to read Psalms and to pray, to cry and to give thanks in the midst of death.

More specifically, our liturgical tradition offers powerful communal practices for grief, such as funerals and memorials, with beautiful prayers for the departed. Our tradition teaches us to grieve in prayer and gesture; we grieve in church and we grieve together. Our prayers are richly healing and show us that Christ knows our suffering, that we are not alone, and that we should pray for our loved ones, just as they continue to pray for us. Further, we grieve not only with prayerful words but also with actions: standing at prayerful attention during a funeral and venerating the deceased's body.

Liturgy as "Not-Forgetting"

It is helpful to frame our analysis from the perspective of liturgical theology. As Fr. Schmemann defined for us, the "primary question is never, 'What do we think about this?,' but rather, 'What is being revealed to us?'—the core question of liturgical theology: How is our very vision and understanding informed and transformed by that experience?"[27] What wisdom and truth is revealed to us in liturgy?

The Orthodox funeral is a sacramental liturgical rite that provides a framework for mourning, celebration, and prayerful contemplation. Its texts and liturgical gestures along with the emphasis on the physical body of the deceased provide a way to contextualize death within our faith in Christ. How is the Orthodox funeral different from other modern-day funerals? How does the presence of the body at the funeral affect our grief? How does revisiting the death in memorial prayers intensify or validate the mourning process?

It is also worth asking a basic question: Who is a funeral for? The dead, the living, or both? It is widely understood in secular society that a funeral is primarily for the living. According to a popular funeral website, the "purpose of funerals" is that they "help us acknowledge that someone we love has died . . . allow us to say goodbye . . . [and] offer continuity and hope for the living."[28] They also "provide a support system for us, friends, family members and the community, [and] allow us to reflect on the meaning of life and death."[29] A person who has expressed no interest in a religious funeral may still have one, if his or her family members are religious and find comfort in prayer. Sometimes the deceased person's requests are respected, but often the most value is placed on the community's grief and on group sharing. In other words, sometimes the secular funeral is both for the deceased and his or her family, but more often than not, it is solely for those who are left behind.

This is not the case with our faith. Instead, the Orthodox funeral is very much for the deceased as well as the bereaved. It is not only a means for those left behind to process their feelings or tell stories, though there is a place for this at the community meal and other informal gatherings. The funeral is a sacrament wherein the deceased *anamnetically* joins us in prayer, lament, and reunion with Christ.

Anamnesis is the word St. Paul uses for "remembrance" when he relates Christ's injunction at the Last Supper to "do this in remembrance of Me" (1 Cor. 11:24). It comes from the Greek word *amnesia*, meaning "loss of memory," plus the prefix "an-," meaning "not." Therefore, we are not only "remembering" the Last Supper when we celebrate liturgy, but we are "not-forgetting" it. This "not-forgetting" has ramifications in terms of grief. Not-forgetting those who have died is woven into the fabric of our lives as Christians.

The Connection to Baptism and the Eucharist

Before exploring the funeral rite itself, we should note how it connects to other sacramental practices of the Church. Deacon Nicholas Denysenko has written on the ways in which Baptism and Eucharist inform and are informed by the funeral rite. He asserts that all "Orthodox liturgy initiates the faithful into a process of death in Christ and dying to themselves, preparing them for eternal life."[30] In a sense, every single liturgical experience is a rehearsal for death and life in Christ.

As our initiation into the body of Christ, the sacrament of baptism "establishes this process of death and dying, and the pattern is repeated in the regular celebration of the Divine Liturgy, and complemented by participation in other liturgical offices."[31] The baptized emerges from the water as a new being, one who has put on Christ. One crucial motif within the blessing of baptismal waters is the profound "inseparability of death and new life."[32] In baptism,

> God recreates those receiving the mystery into new human beings who are God's children, but the process of recreating is impossible without death. The entire human participant needs to be made new, and this process can begin only when the candidate partakes of Christ's death and then puts sin to death.[33]

The anointing with oil, which is imbued with remembrance of God's salvific work for the life of the world, connects a person's daily life with a reminder that "the Christian is expected to continue to die to the temptations of the evil one in continuity with the death to evil inaugurated at Baptism."[34]

Remembrance is also integral to the celebration of the Divine Liturgy. The central commemoration consists of the "Words of Institution, the *Anamnesis* or Memorial, and the *Epiclesis* or invocation of the Holy Spirit."[35] As Fr. Schmemann asserts, "The true unique center and source of that commemoration is the Eucharist. It is not that we find commemoration in the Eucharist, but rather that the Eucharist *per se* is commemoration. It was instituted by Christ as commemoration; 'Do this,' he said, 'in remembrance of me.'"[36] The elements of the anaphora express the "mystery of divine activity accomplished for the life and salvation of all those who seek Christ and who long to be united with Him in eternal communion."[37] The combination of remembrance and prayers for the Holy Spirit remind us that it is not just a single act or intention that unites us in Christ, but the joining of all the elements.

Faithful participation in the Divine Liturgy is a way to keep vigil for the inevitability of death. Liturgical worship offers us a "rehearsal of dying and death for the purpose of rising to new life."[38] Every time we attend liturgy, we are offered a chance to encounter the meaning of the cross, the tomb, and the resurrection on the third day.

Preparing for Holy Communion "shows how death and dying to sin are necessary to receive the gift of communion in the Holy Spirit, which is a foretaste of life shared with the Triune God."[39] Receiving Communion connects us with our life and death in Christ:

> Through the course of the Liturgy, participants engage the practices of death in Christ and dying to sin in preparation for new life. In this sense, the Eucharist is the regular engagement of the process of dying to sin and rising to new life that was initially established at Baptism and fortified at Chrismation.[40]

Denysenko acknowledges the gap between what liturgy reveals and our lived understanding of it as Orthodox Christians. He reflects on the difficult tasks of mystagogy (the interpretation of liturgical mystery), stating, "Even the most sensitive and caring pastor can only do so much to grant the people access to the riches of the liturgical celebration."[41]

And yet we persevere in faithful liturgical practice, which we believe to be the central means of revealing meaning in a world full of life, joy, loss, and mourning. It is neither easy nor pleasant for people to constantly contemplate death. However, if we even glimpse this fullness wherein Christ is revealed to our hearts, we are granted a life-giving vision of God's love for us.

CHAPTER FOUR

The Orthodox Funeral

THE ORTHODOX FUNERAL rite provides a meaningful and powerful opportunity to contemplate death and the promise of eternal life within our parish community. As Fr. Schmemann noted, "What has changed is death itself. Or rather, death has been changed radically—ontologically, if you wish—by Christ's death. Death is no longer a separation, for it has ceased to be separation from God, and thus a separation from life."[42] The texts and hymnography reflect the depth of our relationship to death and life.

We hear Psalms 50/51 and 90/91—hymns of repentance, deliverance, and protection. We pray the refrains together: "Have mercy upon Thy servant."[43] We pray repeatedly, "Give rest, O Lord, to the soul of Thy servant who has fallen asleep."[44] The word "rest" figures prominently in the texts of the funeral, as we pray that our loved one finds eternal rest in Christ. The chanted verses of the idiomela offer spiritual questions, such as "What earthly sweetness remaineth unmixed with grief?" and "What manner of ordeal doth the soul endure when it is parted from the body?" with an emphasis on resting in Christ.[45]

In the funeral service, the evlogetaria for the dead are sung after Psalm 90, with the refrain from Psalm 118: "Blessed art Thou, O Lord, teach me Thy statutes." They are modeled after the evlogetaria of the Resurrection that we sing at matins every Sunday to share the good news of the Resurrection. In the funeral service, however, the texts apply the theme of resurrection to reflect our prayers for the dead and for ourselves, that we may join with Christ in Paradise.[46]

Further, these hymns are sung in the same tone and style as the ones we offer on Sunday mornings: tone five, the resurrectional tone, the tone of the Paschal troparion and stichera. When we experience this music at a funeral, this tone and its melodic patterns bring us into a resurrectional state of mind. This is juxtaposed with other hymns in the funeral service, such as the canon, which are in tone six and thus more evocative of lament and grief.[47]

It is fitting to include the full text of the Epistle and the Gospel. The Epistle exhorts us to grieve with hope that the dead will rise with Christ:

But I do not want you to be ignorant, brethren, concerning those who have fallen asleep, lest you sorrow as others who have no hope. For if we believe that Jesus died and rose again, even so God will bring with Him those who sleep in Jesus. For this we say to you by the word of the Lord, that we who are alive and remain until the coming of the Lord will by no means precede those who are asleep. For the Lord Himself will descend from heaven with a shout, with the voice of an archangel, and with the trumpet of God. And the dead in Christ will rise first. Then we who are alive and remain shall be caught up together with them in the clouds to meet the

Lord in the air. And thus we shall always be with the Lord. (1 Thess. 4:13–17)

The Gospel reading calls us to repentance. We are called to a renewed understanding of God's power and knowledge that those who heed God's call will hear the voice of God:

Most assuredly, I say to you, he who hears My word and believes in Him who sent Me has everlasting life, and shall not come into judgment, but has passed from death into life. Most assuredly, I say to you, the hour is coming, and now is, when the dead will hear the voice of the Son of God; and those who hear will live. For as the Father has life in Himself, so He has granted the Son to have life in Himself, and has given Him authority to execute judgment also, because He is the Son of Man. Do not marvel at this; for the hour is coming in which all who are in the graves will hear His voice and come forth— those who have done good, to the resurrection of life, and those who have done evil, to the resurrection of condemnation. I can of Myself do nothing. As I hear, I judge; and My judgment is righteous, because I do not seek My own will but the will of the Father who sent Me. (John 5:24–30)

This Gospel reading offers a theological teaching about the nature of God and our salvation. It reminds us of judgment and the need for repentance. It shows a vision of resurrection to those who grieve: "He who hears My word . . . shall not come into judgment, but has passed from death into life."

In other prayers, the emphasis is on lamentation:

When death comes, all things are vanished away. . . . Terror truly past compare is by the mystery of death inspired. . . .

Darkness is his (her) dwelling place. . . . Like a blossom that wastes away and like a dream that passes and is gone, so is every mortal into dust resolved. . . . What agony the soul endures when from the body it is parted.[48]

In addition to these vivid descriptions of death, the prayers of the last kiss serve to normalize the crying that accompanies grief and our communal feelings of shock:

Weep, and with tears lament when with understanding I think on death, and see how in the graves there sleeps the beauty which once for us was fashioned in the image of God, but now is shapeless, ignoble, and bare of all the graces. O how strange a thing; what is this mystery which concerns us humans? Why were we given up to decay?[49]

These texts are a call to action and to close contemplation of the heartbreaking situation of loss as it affects the body's beauty: "Come then, let us look closely at the graves; where is the body's beauty? Where the youth? . . . Great the weeping and lamentation; great the weeping and sighing at the parting of the soul!"[50]

These hymns unflinchingly call the grieving attendees to a place of contemplation. We name our sadness and lift it up in prayer: all the feelings, all the pain, all the mystery and strangeness that the one whom we love is now no longer with us. And yet there is no room to get stuck in one emotion or idea; it is all there—lament and joy. The only final word is that of Christ the Word, who trampled down death by death and upon those in the tombs bestowed life.

The liturgical movements and gestures of the clergy indicate a respectful relationship with the deceased. The clergy cense the icons, the body of the departed, and the gathered people, evoking the concept that we are icons of Christ and God's image is imprinted on all of us. The deceased's body is positioned in the center of the church, just as the faithful are at their baptisms and weddings.[51] The deceased's feet face east, oriented toward the direction of Christ's return, in prayer alongside those who have gathered. If the deceased is clergy, there is a sense he is serving liturgy one last time with us on earth before he joins the ongoing heavenly liturgy.

The practice of the last kiss, wherein the gathered may venerate the body of the departed, is a respectful statement of the farewell death brings and of our particular understanding that the body is not to be escaped but integrated into our salvation. We recognize the value of the body as our incarnational faith teaches, and yet we also understand that we are not limited to our bodies. We pray for resurrection in a healed body (1 Cor. 15: 35–44).

We hear multiple voices at the funeral rite. We hear the singing voices of all those gathered, clergy and congregants, together in one prayerful call-and-response to God. We hear the voice of the priest interceding for us while offering consolation and support to the gathered mourners. We also hear the prayerful voice of the deceased speaking to those gathered and to God:

Looking on me as I lie here prone before you, voiceless and unbreathing, mourn for me, everyone; brethren and friends, kindred, and you who knew me well; for but yesterday with you I was talking, and suddenly there came upon me the fearful hour of death: therefore come, all you that long for me, and kiss me with the last kiss of parting. For no longer shall I walk with you, nor talk with you henceforth: for to the Judge I go, where no person is valued for his (her) earthly station. . . . Therefore I beg you all, and implore you, to offer prayer unceasingly for me to Christ our God, that I be not assigned for my sins to the place of torment; but that He assign me to the place where there is Light of Life.[52]

The deceased person is praying and lamenting there with everyone else, attending his or her own funeral. He or she has a voice. He or she is with us. We are reminded that the funeral is truly not only for the bereaved. It is a coming together of all God's people, praying about our ultimate concern—not only the departure of this person from earthly life, but our own repentance, our death, our time in the tomb, our waiting, and our resurrection with Christ.

The Connection to Holy Week and Pascha

The funeral rite at its core evokes the practice of Holy Week. If we do not conceive of Pascha as a single day of resurrection, but instead reflect on Holy Friday, Saturday, and Sunday woven together, we may see Holy Friday as the "Pascha of the cross" and Holy Sunday as the "Pascha of the resurrection."[53] In between, we find the "identification of our death with Holy Saturday."[54] This day has a powerful sense of anticipation, of grief, of vigil, of the "not-yet," and of the anticipatory joy as the vestments change to white. The myrrhbearing women have faithfully arrived, and Christ is not there (Matt. 28:6).

During the Lamentations service held on Friday evening of Holy Week, we set aside time to lament with the Mother of

God. She mourns the death of her only child with a mother's loving grief, with tears and wailing. We hear St. Mary's voice: "I alone, my Child, of all women, gave You birth without pain; now the grief and pain are more than I can endure, at Your suffering."[55] We marvel and grieve with the Theotokos in the same breath: "In a grave they laid thee, O my Life and my Christ: and the armies of the angels were so amazed as they sang the praise of thy submissive love!"[56] We are prayerfully confused by what we see: "How O Life canst thou die? In a grave, how canst thou dwell?"[57] We proclaim a renewed faith: "Right is it indeed, Life-Bestowing Lord, to magnify thee: For upon the cross were thy hands outstretched, and the strength of our dread foe hast thou destroyed."[58]

The words of the Theotokos give voice to every question, every emotion, every possible response to the death of a loved one. We pray these words together with St. Mary, knowing that God hears the cries of our hearts on the deepest level. There is no need to be ashamed of our grief. We live out our grief in the community.

After we have chanted the Lamentations, we sing the evlogetaria from Sunday Matins, albeit in a more somber way. A subtle transformation is occurring: sorrow into joy, death into resurrection. By the time we arrive at the end of the service, the troparia we sang at the beginning of the service are sung again, but this time in a different order.[59] At the beginning of the service, the order is "Pious Joseph," "When Thou didst submit Thyself unto Death (tone two Resurrectional Troparion)," and "Verily the Angel." Toward the end of the service, the tone two Resurrectional Troparion has moved up to the first position, before "Pious Joseph" and "Verily the Angel." We are moving toward the resurrection. We sing "God is the Lord" (normally sung during matins) during the Lamentations service, and this underscores the fact that this "funeral service of Christ" is actually a service of resurrection.[60]

The Orthodox funeral and liturgical texts are not simple platitudes or reassurances; they speak of loss, of being judged by God, of the profound need for prayer and repentance. There is no quick reassurance that everything is fine or that life remains the same. We do not minimize grief or the accompanying state of sorrow and bereavement. We leave room for mystery and contemplation. C. S. Lewis reflects on this state of unknowing in his beautiful book *A Grief Observed*:

> Of course, you can literally believe all that stuff about family reunions "on the further shore," pictured in entirely earthly terms. But that is all unscriptural, all out of bad hymns and lithographs. There's not a word of it in the Bible. And it rings false. We know it couldn't be like that. Reality never repeats. The exact same thing is never taken away and given back. How well the spiritualists bait their hook! "Things on this side are not so different after all." There are cigars in Heaven. For that is what we should all like. The happy past restored.[61]

Instead, our funeral texts honor the surreal and painful feelings of friends and family without implying that soon enough we will all be together smoking cigars, just like old times. The texts underscore the Christian concept of the remembrance of death, as we see in Scripture (1 Cor. 15:31) and in many patristic sources, such as the *Ladder of Divine Ascent*. The prayers encompass everything: death, life, fear, hope, connection, and distance. They hold space for the mystery.

The Orthodox Funeral Homily

The funeral homily is a special opportunity for the priest to provide pastoral care to those gathered in grief. While Orthodox homilies are formal in some ways, due to the structured liturgical setting with set prayers and readings, there is still a great deal of flexibility in that the priest chooses how to speak about the deceased within the context of our life in Christ.

The Orthodox funeral homily is not the time to focus solely on stories of the deceased. And though it may be tempting to seize the opportunity for evangelization (seeing as the church may be filled with people who do not normally attend the parish), this is also not the point of the funeral homily. Instead, the homily is an opportunity to offer a thoughtful reflection on the life of the departed person while framing his or her life—and *all* of our lives—in the greater context of repentance, joy, mercy, and forgiveness. Christ is the center of the funeral, and insofar as we have "put on Christ" in our baptisms, those gathered find their center in Him.

For this section, I draw on Hans Boersma's writing on St. Gregory of Nyssa's funeral homilies, as well as helpful conversations with two wise priests from St. Vladimir's Orthodox Theological Seminary, Fr. Nicholas Solak and Fr. Sergius Halvorsen.

An effective homily is first and foremost connected to the overall liturgical context. It is not a break from the liturgy. Instead, the words, tone, and content amplify aspects of our

Christian worship. A homily is not a chance to tell stories that draw one's attention to the homilist, nor is it an opportunity to synthesize all Christian theology in ten minutes. We must "focus and simplify," as Fr. Halvorsen so often says to his homiletics students. The purpose of a homily is to offer consolation and compassion, to turn us toward Christ with hope.

The tone of the funeral homily is one with which we should be familiar. It is a tone of bright sadness, of joyful sorrow; it is the tone we know as we contemplate both Crucifixion and Resurrection. Anyone who has moved through the liturgical year knows that we hold these seemingly conflicting concepts together. The tone must be humble and prayerful, holding space for sorrow as well as hope.

As the Christian writer Justin Brierly notes, it is "important to remember that people who are actually going through suffering need our love, not our logic. They need someone to sit and weep with them, not to present a . . . sermon on why God allows evil."[62] It is not the place to attempt a theological reflection on theodicy. Instead, we are called to grieve together as the Church, as Christ's Body, and to remember that we are praying for repose "where sickness, sorrow and sighing have fled away and where the sight of Your countenance rejoices all the saints."[63] We are praying that the deceased may repose in a place of rest in Christ.

REMEMBERING THE DECEASED

The priest may know the deceased very well, or may never have met the person, or may have a connection in between these two extremes. This is a particular pastoral opportunity and challenge. In my work as a hospice chaplain, I have officiated at dozens of Christian memorial services for people I had never met because they were already close to death at the time of hospice admission. I realized quite early in my practice that I should never try to eulogize as if I had intimate knowledge of the deceased. I would run the risk of saying something wrong or missing something important. Also, it is not a time to share the person's biography. Instead, I gather as much information as I can but leave the specifics to others to share, whether in a toast afterward or in short reflections during the service.

There is a tension here: as Fr. Halvorsen reminds us, a funeral is a service in which we commend a specific person into the hands of God. The task of the funeral sermon is not to canonize the departed, and yet the sermon must say *something* about the deceased. Father Halvorsen noted, "The most effective way to do this is to examine the ways in which we were able to see the power of God, the love of Christ, and the grace of the Holy Spirit in the life of the departed. What were unique facets of his or her life that enable us to hear more perfectly the Word of God?"[64] How may we connect the person's life to our ongoing perception of God's love and mercy among His people?

Father Nicholas Solak also noted in conversation that in a sense, a funeral homily is half *eulogy* (literally, "a good word") and half *kerygma* (literally, a "proclamation" which, in our context, is about Christ). Father Solak observed that we often say good things about the deceased and their families but may pass over the obvious shortcomings of the deceased. He noted, "Whereas there is a certain and important aspect of compassion in that, it is also a bit out of step with the overriding spirit of the funeral service," which includes repeated reminders of repentance and forgiveness.[65] Father Solak wondered if it is better to offer something like, "Joe was a good guy in many ways, but Joe was human like all of us . . . and we are here to begin forgiving and asking forgiveness as he stands before the Lord."[66] Father Halvorsen similarly reflected on this tension, saying, "It is inappropriate to make the departed seem as though they lived a sinless life, and if the departed had specific struggles well known to the community, these can be alluded to—for example, 'We all knew that Pete was not perfect.'"[67] But this should be offered in a gentle way that "acknowledges the reality without being condemning."[68]

I, too, have navigated this seeming paradox; for example, I once officiated at a nondenominational Christian memorial service for a hospice patient who was well known to be a curmudgeon, to put it mildly. His elderly wife sat in her wheelchair at his gravesite after we finished the service. As she looked at the bundles of purple irises atop her husband's grave, she said tearfully, "Ron was a miserable jerk. But at least he was *my* miserable jerk." This comment brilliantly encapsulates the complexity of grief, especially when a survivor may have had a complicated or fraught relationship with the deceased. The departed lived and died—imperfectly, humanly—in relationships that were complex. And he or she is still missed, and still loved, despite the misery he or she may have caused. We do not need to insult the departed, but we do well to acknowledge that he or she wasn't perfect, and neither are we. The only perfect person is Christ, and as we turn toward Him, we see our imperfections as well as a model of hope and full humanity.

THE HOMILY'S ROLE IN EMOTIONAL SUPPORT

As we have discussed, St. Gregory of Nyssa was critical of his personal grief and judged it against the passions and the rational mind. However, when he gave funeral homilies, he did not subject his parishioners to quite the same judgment.

It is perhaps the *liturgical context* of the funeral that allows St. Gregory to soften and nuance his critique. In several funeral orations, he "actively encourages the congregation to give full voice to their sense of loss."[69] At the funeral of Bishop Meletius in 381, he states, "Is it not rather that I reach not the full extent of our loss, though I exceed in the loudness of my expression of grief? Lend me, oh lend me, my brethren, the tear of sympathy."[70] At the funeral of the young princess Pulcheria, St. Gregory publicly laments, "Who passed by the calamity without groaning? Who did not bemoan the loss of life? Who has not shed tears at the calamity? Who has not mingled his own voice with the common funeral lament?"[71] In the year 386, at the funeral of the Empress Flacilla, St. Gregory notes how those gathered, as well as the clouds, are "weeping gentle drops."[72] These examples show us how St. Gregory preaches in a pastorally sensitive manner. The first half of his funeral orations addresses the physical and emotional experiences of grief, as quoted above, and the second makes a transition toward consolation and hope in Christ.

When grief is expressed within liturgy, the bereaved may move authentically toward a fuller understanding of the consolation of heaven. Perhaps the funeral setting empowers St. Gregory—and all those who eulogize the departed—to let go of false distinctions. The funeral contains it all: hope, crying, joy, resurrection, crucifixion, humility, and silence. There is no need for the priest to pit reason and emotion against each other. Instead, it is appropriate and pastorally compassionate to acknowledge the tremendous power of grief and the even greater power of Christ.

Indeed, the funeral homily holds powerful opposites in a dialectical tension. For example, one might emphasize that God is both *here*, on earth, and *there*, in heaven. Father Halvorsen notes that the common trap of overemphasizing heaven may "[imply] that the Kingdom of Heaven is not eternal" and not present here with us.[73] Yes, we hope the departed will be embraced by the Lord after death, but too much emphasis can "imply that this Lord is otherwise absent from our lives," and thus amplify the loss.[74] We must not forget that God is *here with those who are grieving*: "If death is all about looking forward to *finally* encountering Christ, who is otherwise absent, this leaves the grieving in a particularly difficult situation, since not only are they deprived of the physical presence of the departed, but they are faced with the implied message that Christ is not present for us today in our grief!"[75] We may discuss the ways God has been present in the life of the departed. This will remind the gathered that Christ is present for those of us who are grieving, here and now.

Other tensions inherent in grief may also be touched on in the homily. First, grief can be isolating, yet we grieve together as a community, standing and praying in union with each other. The grieving ones feel the quiet and deep sadness of loss while trying to manage all the busy practical details of the funeral, burial, and gathering family members. The homilist himself may be grieving as well, if he knew the person; hence he must allow for his own sorrow while managing the sorrow of others. The funeral feels quite final—it is the last time loved ones can see the deceased's body—and yet it is just the beginning of grief. Those who are grieving are called to trust God, but what they might want to do most is to question God.

There are no easy answers. But again, the funeral homily offers us an opportunity to remember that we do not understand everything. We look to Christ and trust His mercy. As Fr. Halvorsen reminds us, "Ultimately, God will reveal how the death of a loved one is in fact according to God's providential will; however, this is a conclusion that the hearer needs to come to personally. Attempting to resolve this mystery in the funeral at best will sound superficial, and at worst will sound callous."[76] In the funeral homily, we cannot resolve all questions of grief, but we can rest in the truth we confess as Christ's Body: that Christ is in our midst.

The Practice of Memorials

Another powerful aspect of liturgical life is the holding of memorials on the third day (often coinciding with the funeral), the ninth day, the fortieth day, and annually thereafter.[77] What a practical way to revisit our grief in the safety of the Church! The Church understands that we need these periodic moments to pause our busy lives, to stop and pray, to cry and remember. The memorial services are the Church's way of telling us that we should regularly acknowledge the life and death of our loved ones. We check in with our grief as it changes and heals.

Saint Symeon of Thessaloniki interprets the timing of memorials in a spiritual way:

The third day Memorial we do for the Holy Trinity, because from the Holy Trinity we have our existence and our life. The ninth day Memorials remind us of the nine orders of holy Angels, among which our beloved one has been numbered. The fortieth day Memorial is for the Ascension of our Savior.[78]

Memorials are an opportunity to revisit a grief that is already present. This tradition nudges us to refocus on our loved one, to stand together and pray. It is a chance for the parish to hold a grieving family in prayer. It is a chance to invite reflection on the deceased's life and death and a reminder to check on the bereaved family. Often, the family of the memorialized person will have a special place at the front of the congregation. Some parishes formalize this even more: at the end of the service, after venerating the cross, the parishioners walk by the family and offer a handshake, a hug, and their condolences. It is similar to a receiving line at a wedding and is offered inside the church.

These memorials are a chance for all those present to contemplate the fact that one day, someone else (God willing) will sing "May her memory be eternal" about us. This practice disrupts the common and awkward dance around the subject of grief, in which we wonder if we should mention someone's death to a family member lest we upset them. Memorials are a liturgical reinforcement of the value of touching on the pain of loss, a pain that often lies barely beneath the surface. It is a release of tears, an experience of supportive community, and a reminder that a loved one's memory remains eternal. The Church teaches us how to grieve.

A Vision for the Community

Though the practice of memorials is an important communal practice of prayerfully revisiting grief, there is room for improvement in bereavement care within our churches. Some churches have pastoral visitation programs, but this is not common.

Therese Lysaught has written extensively and persuasively on dying, grief, and bereavement care. In her work "Geographies and Accompaniment," she offers an excellent overview and analysis of the changing physical locations and theoretical frameworks for death and dying. Most notably, she offers suggestions for a reimagining of the ancient order of widows or order of accompaniment, wherein widows would be blessed to provide grief support to members of the community:

> By incorporating eligible widows—those bereft of husbands, children and grandchildren and therefore in peril socially and economically—into the ministerial structure of the community, the Church provided significant material assistance for the most vulnerable members of the community. It also recognized and lifted up their practice of discipleship and continued to utilize their talents and abilities in service of the Church's mission.[79]

This ministry met a need within the community, using the natural gifts of these women. Their responsibilities varied; they offered ceaseless prayer on behalf of the community, visiting the sick, especially sick women. They offered practical instruction to younger women within their communities along with presence in the parish.

What a visionary and practical way to use the talents of these women while honoring an unmet need! The ministry of widows illustrates to us that one who has been through loss may be particularly gifted at caring for those in a similar situation, and so this concept is worth addressing in such a program. We would do well to consider a program such as this—and I should mention, perhaps it could be opened to non-widows. Perhaps it could include any qualified and gifted member of a parish, including counselors, chaplains, or others with gifts of caregiving.

Memory Found within Community

In her poem, "Blessing of Memory," the writer Jan Richardson notes how profound is the memory of a departed loved one. And yet, if the day comes when the bereaved can no longer bear to remember, the community's collective knowing can be a reminder of a loved one's gifts.[80] It is within the sacramental life of the Church, from baptism to Holy Communion and the sacrament of the funeral, that Orthodox Christians may be assured of being remembered. We find rest in the Church, the Body of Christ. We hear the deeply familiar memorial prayers we offer as one body:

> With the spirits of the righteous made perfect, give rest to the soul of Thy servant, O Savior; and preserve it in that life of blessedness which is with thee, O thou who lovest mankind. In the place of Thy rest O Lord, where all Thy Saints repose, give rest also to the soul of Thy servant; for Thou only lovest

mankind. Thou art our God, who descended into Hell, and loosed the bonds of those who were there; Thyself give rest also to the soul of Thy servant. O Virgin, alone pure and immaculate, who without stain didst bring forth God, intercede for the salvation of his soul. May their memory be eternal.[81]

We have inherited a profound gift of liturgical prayer and gesture, a gift that unites the deceased and the bereaved in the Body of Christ. Our liturgy affirms our deepest instincts to grieve together as a community, with joy and sorrow, tears and silence. We stand still in contemplation and we walk and move in ways that honor both the living and the dead as members of the Body of Christ. As we pray together, singing in joyful sorrow born of grief, we embody our belief that Christ knows our suffering and transforms it through His life, death, and resurrection. Christ is Risen!

Living and Grieving as Orthodox Christians

CHAPTER FIVE

Grieving in the Modern World

A S CHRISTIANS, WE are immersed in a diverse cultural framework as we work, study, and navigate our daily lives. For many reasons, grief has become part of the public dialogue more than ever. A variety of non-Orthodox bereavement resources is available at our fingertips, from books and retreats to self-help groups. We grieve with others increasingly on social media, with tribute pages and even online memorial services. Certainly, some of the existing secular bereavement resources can be helpful. They are not sufficient to fully support Christians in grief, but certain theories and concepts can be meaningful when linked to a life of faith. Thus, it is valuable to examine these approaches to grief and determine how these attitudes may affect our bereavement.

Defining Our Terms

It will be helpful to define our terms: Loss is the condition of being deprived or bereaved of something or someone, or the disappearance of something cherished.[82] A person may suffer a crisis of self, personhood, identity, and/or relationship in the wake of loss. One may experience a crisis of faith in response to loss; our clergy are certainly familiar with this tendency.

Grief is the normal response to loss. It is multifaceted and complex, and involves an ongoing process of constructing meaning in a world that has been changed by loss. Grief encompasses the physiological, psychological, and behavioral responses that occur due to bereavement.[83]

Bereavement is an objective state of having lost someone or something; it is associated with the specific event of loss.[84]

Finally, mourning is the process by which someone adapts to a loss; it is considered to be the outward expression of the loss.[85] Mourning is a process, and it is profoundly influenced by culture.[86] Cultural norms for mourning may include, for example, the practice of wearing black, particular ways of mourning in public, adhering to behavior expected of the bereaved, and other culturally situated practices. Mourning begins at the time of death and may continue for an undefined period of time.

Mourning can occur even before the death of a loved one, as we see with "anticipatory grief"—the grief experienced before the death of a terminally ill person. Anticipatory grief may affect the dying person and his or her loved ones. Its emotional intensity fluctuates and is confusing, as it can create a sense of wondering, "Why am I grieving now, while my loved one is still alive?" We may see anticipatory grief in the experience of families and friends of those afflicted with Alzheimer's disease or other forms of dementia, along with other slowly progressing diseases. This is important to know because if a person has been grieving during a slowly progressing illness, he or she may arrive at a loved one's funeral in a different emotional place than if the death had been sudden or traumatic. Acknowledging and even facilitating the sharing of anticipatory grief can improve the overall experience of grief and mourning.[87]

Systematizing Grief

The mid-twentieth-century psychiatrist Dr. Erich Lindemann is often credited with the first attempts to "medicalize" the grief process. He describes an acute phase, consisting of physical symptoms and numbness, and a second phase, including anger, preoccupation, guilt, and isolation. Lindemann introduced the concept that grieving should take about one year. Frankly, our society is still trying to recover from that potentially damaging idea.[88] This concept is notably different from an Orthodox viewpoint, because our practice of periodic memorials and our conception of "memory eternal" challenge any notion that grief adheres to a structured human timeline.

For Dr. Lindemann, after these initial phases, the grief recedes, new life patterns are formed, and the bereaved person eventually "gets over it." The goal of getting over grief is still unfortunately "the unquestioned and unequivocal desire of all who deal with the bereaved, and indeed of all groups in American society today."[89] This concept of getting over loss has permanently affected society's approach to grief, and it is to be resisted by Christians living with a broader vision of life and death. Resisting can be difficult, of course, but we have Holy Tradition to rely on. Indeed, as noted earlier, the Orthodox liturgical cycle reminds us that grief is cyclical and is revisited over the course of the mourner's life in memorials and the endless prayers of "memory eternal."

In 1969, the "stages of dying" were developed by Dr. Elizabeth Kubler-Ross to explore the possible phases experienced by a terminally ill person anticipating his or her own death. Over time, these stages were increasingly applied to understanding grief and mourning. In 2004, Dr. Kubler-Ross expanded these categories into "stages of grieving." It is undeniable that Dr. Kubler-Ross's work has shaped the dialogue of grief work in many positive ways, but its ongoing limitations are also well documented.[90] She has given us helpful terminology, but again, grief does not always fall neatly into categories.

The psychologist Dr. William Worden described grief as a series of nonlinear tasks to be "worked through." His four tasks involved accepting the reality of the loss, experiencing the pain of grief, adjusting to a different type of environment, and finally, emotionally relocating the loss and moving on with life.[91] The fourth edition of Worden's book amended the last task of mourning to "finding an enduring connection with the deceased in the midst of embarking on a new life."[92]

Dr. Therese Rando created the "6-R process" of mourning: recognize the loss, react to the separation, recollect the deceased and the relationship, relinquish the old attachments to the deceased and the assumptive world, readjust to move adaptively into the new world without forgetting the old, and reinvest.[93] Based on her work, the predominant therapeutic stances began to focus more on acceptance of the loss, closure, and eventual reinvestment of the bereaved person's energy. The intention was to create a new life and a new sense of self.

It is helpful to note this shift of terminology: from stages, to tasks, to processes. Grief began to be described as more active and less confined in its relation to time. Other practitioners of grief therapeutic models also shape our current attitudes, including Dr. Alan Wolfelt and Dr. Kenneth Doka. Doka altered the professional conversation with his term "disenfranchised grief," which is response to a loss that is not socially supported or acknowledged, as well as his concepts of "instrumental" and "intuitive" types of grief.[94]

Grieving with Others

Alan Wolfelt beautifully describes the value of compassionate grief support in his "Understanding Your Grief Support Group Guide."[95] He cautions the reader to remember the limits of the medical model of caregiving. This model, as noted above, asserts that the primary goal of bereavement is "a series of completed tasks, extinguished pain, and the establishment of new relationships."[96] This model of grief uses a "recovery or resolution definition to suggest a return to 'normalcy.'"[97] But Wolfelt reminds us that a person's life is changed forever after the death of a loved one. The loss remains, and closure is never quite achieved; instead, the bereaved person learns to relocate his or her loved one in a different place in the heart. To me, Wolfelt stands out from other secular grief theorists by presenting a holistic model of living with grief.[98]

The Diversity of Resources on Grief

In my work as a chaplain to patients of different religious backgrounds, I am often asked for grief resources from a secular perspective. Some of these resources reflect on valuable themes of loss, identity, relationships, and healing. For example, Wolfelt's ten "Touchstones" encourage the reader to:

1. open to the presence of loss;
2. dispel misconceptions about grief;
3. embrace the uniqueness of your grief;
4. explore your feelings of loss;
5. recognize you are not crazy;
6. understand the six needs of mourning;
7. nurture yourself;
8. reach out for help;
9. seek reconciliation; and
10. appreciate your transformation.[99]

Joanne Cacciatore's *Bearing the Unbearable* is a moving account of the wisdom she has accumulated both as a professional grief counselor and as a bereaved parent. For children's grief, I recommend *Lifetimes*,[100] *The Butterfly Field*,[101] *Tear Soup*,[102] and *The Invisible String*,[103] but they are notably secular.

As helpful as these resources are, even the most thoughtful secular approach cannot touch the depths of everyone's grief. For example, if forgiveness is a key aspect of someone's grief, there are major differences between the way a nonreligious person might conceptualize grief and the way a Christian might. I imagine someone could come to a place of moderately healthy forgiveness without the foundation of the Church. But how much more complete is forgiveness when it is seen holistically, within a life in Christ, a life of prayer and sacramental worship? We are taught to forgive as God forgives us; we pray for forgiveness and continual mercy; we recall how Christ taught us to forgive "seventy times seven" times. We confess that healing from grief connects to the One who heals, the One who consoles. Ultimately, any secular attempts to support grief are only partially helpful. The most complete grief support draws meaning from a life of faith.

CHAPTER SIX

Continuing Bonds

THE GRIEF THEORY that resonates best with a vision for Orthodox Christian bereavement is the concept of continuing bonds. In 1996, Klass, Silverman, and Nickman wrote a pivotal book entitled *Continuing Bonds: New Understandings of Grief*, in which they proposed a new model for bereavement that took into account an ongoing relationship with the deceased.[104] Drawing on attachment theory, the concept of continuing bonds denotes "the presence of an ongoing inner relationship with the deceased person by the bereaved individual."[105] This model is much less linear than those previously proposed. It moved away from concepts such as working through grief or arriving at a place wherein one's grief is fully resolved.

The concept of continuing bonds has recently had a strong resurgence in psychological and mental health literature. Continuing bonds are increasingly understood to be a norm and not an exception. The research indicates they can be positive and comforting in the grief process. For example, forgiveness may facilitate healing within the process of continuing bonds; notably, continuing bonds in the context of spirituality may facilitate post-traumatic growth.[106] It is certainly within the realm of Christian belief to have meaningful connections, such as dreams or prayerful moments, with deceased loved ones. The concept underlying continuing bonds is obvious to many Orthodox people, as I learned during my interviews with the grieving, which I share in the coming chapters.

It is natural for Orthodox Christians to remain connected to the dead, to pray for the dead, to ask the dead to intercede for us, and to live in a manner that honors and interacts with the dead. It is not a mental stretch for us to conceptualize grief in this way, whether praying for our loved ones at bedtime, naming them in memorials, or seeing them in dreams. We set up icon corners with candles in our homes to pray for the saints and ask for their prayers. We feel connected to special saints whose names we give to our loved ones. We name babies after departed loved ones; our names have meaning, and they connect us to those who have gone before us.

As Christians, we can see that continuing bonds are common, meaningful, and even healthy as a person copes with the loss of a loved one. We see these bonds within Scripture: "For God so loved the world that He gave His only begotten Son, that whoever believes in Him should not perish but have everlasting life" (John 3:16). This promise of eternal life means that we do not perish. We do not disappear forever or cease to exist. Instead, through Christ, we gain eternal life in our death.

We profess, "For if we believe that Jesus died and rose again, even so God will bring with Him those who sleep in Jesus" (1 Thess. 4:14). Further, we have the great testament to Christ's salvific and eternal bonds contained in the Paschal Homily of

St. John Chrysostom. Saint John joyfully proclaims to us, "O death, where is thy sting? . . . Christ is risen, and the angels rejoice! Christ is risen, and life reigns! Christ is risen, and not one dead remains in a tomb! For Christ, being raised from the dead, has become the First-fruits of them that have slept."[107] Truly, as we hear these words each year on Pascha, let us marvel at how powerful, relevant, and meaningful they are.

As Fr. Schmemann noted, the "relationship between the deceased and the living is primarily that of communion, of an indestructible unity in Christ. . . . Death is no longer a separation."[108] In other words, the dead remain connected to the living because they, too, are alive. We prayerfully say "Memory eternal" on the occasion of a loved one's death, and we continue saying this for as long as we need. We do not say, "Memory for the next thirteen months," or "Memory until you're ready to move on." The person remains in God's eternal memory and in ours.

Every act of living and breathing as an Orthodox Christian is an act of continuing bonds. Whether praying for the dead as a family or standing in prayer at a memorial for a parish member, we are acting in love for those who have passed. As Fr. Anthony Coniaris of blessed memory notes in *Surviving the Loss of a Loved One*, Christianity is a religion of love, and "praying for the dead is an expression of love. We ask God to remember our departed because we love them. Love relationships survive death and even transcend it."[109] Acknowledging our continuing bonds is an act of love. Our prayers for those who have died are acts of love.

As Fr. Schmemann explains, it is "human love, but also the divine love that God poured into all hearts, Christ's love by which we pray not only for our own, despite our sadness, but also for those whom God loves and makes into the object of our love."[110] As my colleague Dean Theophilos once noted at an Orthodox conference, "Want to grieve together? Let's have communion together, let's go to Church together. The reality of the Eucharist is a continuing bond because we are united in Christ, with those who have fallen asleep."[111] We benefit from understanding the concept of continuing bonds, because it makes sense within our inherited tradition. We give name to what is already there. We pray for our loved ones, and we rest together in Christ.

CHAPTER SEVEN

The Real Face of Grief

There is no remedy for love but to love more.

—HENRY DAVID THOREAU

Let us agree for now that we will not say the breaking makes us stronger or that it is better to have this pain than to have done without this love. Let us promise we will not tell ourselves time will heal the wound, when every day our waking opens it anew. Perhaps for now it can be enough to simply marvel at the mystery of how a heart so broken can go on beating, as if it were made for precisely this—as if it knows the only cure for love is more of it, as if it sees the heart's sole remedy for breaking is to love still, as if it trusts that its own persistent pulse is the rhythm of a blessing we cannot begin to fathom but will save us nonetheless.[112]

—JAN RICHARDSON

IN THIS SECTION, I will share with you some stories I have collected from Orthodox Christians who were grieving. But before we get into the stories, I want to take this chapter to encourage you to take special care of yourself at this time and to face your grief on your own terms, not in the way others expect of you.

You may be wondering, "How will I ever feel peace again?" or "Am I going crazy?" You may wonder, "Am I normal?" or "Is it okay to be angry at God?" You may feel numb or overwhelmed. You may feel disconnected from others or even from God.

You may think, "I don't know if I will ever be the same." And the truth is, you will probably never be the same. Grief changes you. But when you give grief the attention and loving care it needs, you will make it through. It takes time and gentleness and patience. You should treat your heart, body, and mind with extra care and compassion.

The truth is, grief is not pretty. It's not as graceful as it looks in the movies: gazing out the window at a sunset, with a single tear rolling down your cheek. Instead, grief looks more like ugly crying in the line at the grocery store because a woman there reminds you of your mother. Grief looks like having to excuse yourself from joyful events to have a brief crying session alone in the bathroom. It's leaving your phone in the freezer, or trying to open your front door with your automatic car keys, or staring blankly at a wall. All of this is normal.

Repeat this with me: *The only way out of deep grief is through it.* What this means is that you need to give yourself the time and space to process it. You need to allow God to love you the way you are, with all your worries, and hopes, and fears. You will hear how others have done this successfully. It is not selfish to do this. It is deeply necessary.

There are many practical aspects to coping with grief. These include getting extra sleep, talking one-on-one to a therapist, connecting with special trusted friends, eating healthy foods, prioritizing your spiritual practices, praying, and doing small things that bring you joy. Please remember to prioritize your health if you are newly grieving. Consult with your physician if you find that you are not sleeping or you are having health problems. Are you suddenly immersing yourself in work? Or avoiding activities you used to enjoy? Eating significantly more or less, drinking too much alcohol? Engaging in risky behaviors or spending too much money? Again, I prayerfully ask that you prioritize your health, both mental and physical. Try to tell your loved ones and friends what you need, setting boundaries around your time and energy as you see fit.

There are also deeper, more internal aspects to grief: thinking through who you are now, where you want to be, how you want to spend this next chapter of your life, and how you are going to move through your emotions. We will address these questions in the next sections.

One issue almost every grieving person encounters within the first year of loss is how to get through the holidays. If you can't bear to face the first holidays without your loved one, you have full permission to try something different. A great example of this is my dear friend who lost her mother to cancer many years ago. As she and her siblings approached the first holiday season without their mother—without her incredible cooking and uncontrollable laugh and familiar love—they made a group decision to skip their normal traditions altogether. Instead, they went to Florida, swam with dolphins, and attended holiday services there. They gave themselves permission to do something different. And by the next time the holidays rolled around, they were ready to be together again, to think about building new traditions within their family. They will always miss their mother. Now they light a candle for her each year, and they enjoy making some of her best recipes.

When I was growing up, my grandmother, Mary Byrne, always hosted Christmas Day festivities. She had nine children and many grandchildren. Christmas Day was always a boisterous celebration with kids running around, hymns by the piano, dogs knocking things over, crumpled wrapping paper on the floor, lots of chips and dip, and the yearly realization that the turkey probably should have been put in the oven several hours earlier. It was chaos, and we loved it. When my grandmother passed away, our family had to regroup and figure out what to do. It was too much for any one of the aunts and uncles to host the Christmas chaos. So we chose to meet at a local Catholic retreat center and have a meal catered. It was different, yes—but it was beautiful and fun in a new way. Grandma would have been proud. Actually, I'm sure she is proud.

Maybe you want to keep some traditions going, such as familiar cooking or baking. Maybe it is time to start new traditions that focus on loving and caring for others: dropping off toys to children in the hospital, bringing food to a food bank, or giving out warm socks to the homeless. You have permission to choose what works for you, and I encourage you to think broadly about new holiday traditions. Remember, we encounter

Christ's healing presence when we care for others and allow them to care for us.

I love the words of Ted Loder, from his book *Guerrillas of Grace*: "O God, make of me some nourishment for these starved times, some food for my brothers and sisters who are hungry for gladness and hope, that being bread for them, I may also be fed and be full." How beautiful! Let us "be bread" for others. Perhaps most importantly, try to stay connected to your church community. If it feels awkward or painful to attend church by yourself, reach out to a friend or church member to stand next to you. You can do it. God is with us.

CHAPTER EIGHT

The Early Days of Grieving

IN THE FOLLOWING chapters, I invite you to listen deeply to the voices of fellow grieving Orthodox Christians. As part of my research for this book, I interviewed twenty grieving Orthodox people who graciously and bravely shared their stories, questions, and insights with me. To protect the identities of my participants, I assigned new names to all those quoted here.

The participants ranged in age from twenty-nine to seventy-one. Their backgrounds included two Jewish people who had converted to Christianity, seven Caucasians of mixed heritage, one Black American, one Ethiopian, one Egyptian, one Greek, one Cypriot, one White Anglo-Saxon (former) Protestant, two Lebanese, one Romanian, one Russian, and one Polish-German. I interviewed eight members of the Antiochian Orthodox Archdiocese of North America, three members of the Armenian Apostolic Church, one member of the Bulgarian Orthodox Church, two members of the Greek Orthodox Archdiocese of America, and six members of the Orthodox Church in America.

Eight participants are converts, and twelve were raised

Orthodox Christian. The relationships of the deceased to the participants included husband, wife, father, mother, sibling, friend, and child. The child losses included an adult son and unborn babies (one woman with multiple miscarriages). I interviewed five people whose departed loved ones were not Orthodox; the rest had Orthodox loved ones.

I hope these chapters will normalize some of your grief experiences and provoke reflection and insight. I invite you to hear these grieving people's stories and their words with an open heart. Perhaps they will resonate with your own thoughts.

Real Stories: The Initial Reaction to Loss

We experience varying levels of distress and intense reactions at the time of loss. My interviewee Quinn said, "[My dear friend's death] was deeply distressing. There's this sense that when there are people in the world with you, you're okay and the world is in balance. You have a perception that the presence of a righteous soul is balancing out the fallenness of the world. And when they're not there, it's a big loss. You have to readjust." Chris stated, "Grief is so isolating. I had an immediate sense of unreality. I felt like Job." Leonard said his father's death was "the worst thing that ever happened to [him]."

Sometimes we find ourselves in a state of disconnection, and our reactions feel different from the reactions of family members or friends. For Olga, "It was a shock. My cousins didn't react like I did. I just cried and cried. It was so painful." Mark stated simply, "I was in shock. [The day my brother died] was the worst day of my life. I was trying to help my parents cry, but they were basically absent." Did you feel alone in your early days of grief? Do you still feel that way?

Leonard wondered if his faith prevented him from having any immediate emotional reaction. "Maybe I was too focused on him going to heaven that I didn't cry right away." Bonnie said, "I was in go mode." She was focused on the practical details of the death: contacting the funeral home, arranging services, calling family members. Mark, too, felt that "there was so much to do." Leonard and Mark eventually had strong emotional reactions, but their initial reactions were outwardly calm.

Priscilla's initial reaction to the loss was framed by the liturgical time of year: "She died on Holy Monday. It was during Bridegroom matins! Our parish was praying for her when she died. It was such a blessing. I was so comforted!" Elena's first instinct, after hearing of the sudden loss of her son, was to turn to a familiar faith practice: "I immediately went to my icon corner to pray with my family. That was the first thing I did." It was a comfort to have a place of prayer and refuge at the time of loss.

Real Stories: Emotions Are Tunnels

In their book *Burnout*, Emily and Amelia Nagoski share a brilliant concept: "Emotions are tunnels. You have to go all the way through the darkness to get to the light at the end."[113] The profound, life-altering event of losing a loved one activates the stress response in the body. In order to process this stress, we need to face it from all angles: mental, spiritual, and physical. We are whole people.

The best way to address emotional stress, oddly enough, is physical exercise: running, dancing, wrestling with your kids, swimming, anything. We also need to be attuned to our mental and spiritual needs and meet them through prayer, conversation, laughter, physical affection, and social interaction.

During a time of bereavement, we may get stuck in stressful emotions such as sadness, shame, anger, or fear. Perhaps we can hide from those feelings for a while, but they will come out eventually—whether that means we snap angrily at someone who doesn't deserve it, or start bawling our eyes out about something insignificant, or walk around with our shoulders hunched up around our ears. When a stressful emotion comes up, we need to notice it in the moment in order to fully let it happen and to fully let it go.

Let's try not to judge or shame ourselves for having emotions. Just look at the Psalms: "Save me, O God! For the waters have come up to my neck. I sink in deep mire, where there is no standing; I have come into deep waters, where the floods overflow me. I am weary with my crying; my throat is dry; my eyes fail while I wait for my God" (Ps. 69:1–3). These ancient words are refreshingly honest. How many people have chanted these lamentations before us?

The Psalms give voice to the real pain of loss while helping us remember to trust in God. This interplay of sadness and rejoicing is a theme throughout the Psalms. Psalm 13, for example, begins with sorrow: "How long, O Lord? Will You forget me forever? How long will You hide Your face from me? How long shall I take counsel in my soul, Having sorrow in my heart daily?" (Ps. 13:1, 2) The psalm circles back to the theme of trust and patience: "But I have trusted in Your mercy; My heart shall rejoice in Your salvation. I will sing to the Lord, Because He has dealt bountifully with me" (Ps. 13:5–6). Consider reading through one psalm every day as a way to give voice to your struggles. If you are stuck and need a good cry, play a song that evokes memories or watch a reliable tear-jerker of a movie to get those tears out.

The emotions a bereaved person feels can be overwhelming and exhausting. Kate said she was a "mix of emotions," but also, "There was so much grace. There was a lot of beauty and peace. I'm thankful I had time to prepare and that my husband received communion before he died. I was borne up by the prayers." These prayers gave her reassurance and hope that she and her husband were surrounded by God's love.

Daria stated, "I just miss [my dear friend]. I cry for selfishness. I wish he was still here." Elena's experience "wasn't anger at God. It was just generalized anger that [my son struggling with addiction] was so broken." Gabi said, "I was so tired, I kept forgetting everything, making small mistakes, just so out of it!" Grief can cause a person to feel "in a fog," as Gabi felt. Chris "felt weightless, cut off" from his friends and family. Quinn said, "The sorrow was mine. It wasn't for [my friend who had died]. She was fine. I wasn't." Quinn's faith reassured her that her friend was in a place of peaceful rest, even if Quinn and her family were in a state of sadness and loss.

Real Stories: Reactions of Friends and Family

Friends and family may offer both helpful and unhelpful words of consolation. Hazel said, "People will tell you to move on. Never listen to them. Savor all that you had. It's a gift!" A different friend reminded her to take as long she needed, which helped Hazel a great deal. Leonard said, "Honestly it was hard, because at my dad's funeral and wake, everyone kept saying that I seemed fine and good, and it was like I was comforting them. People were surprised I had a smile on my face. But I think it's because I was in shock."

Priscilla's mom was in her late nineties when she died. Priscilla said, "Everyone kept saying, she had a long life. It's true, but it doesn't really matter how old she was or how long she lived. She's still my mom!" She was not comforted by their words because her grief was still profound. You may find that people say unhelpful things, though they are trying to help you while comforting themselves.

Bonnie's friend said to her, "This is a mystery: life and death. Sometimes we need help crossing that bridge. You take as long as you need to grieve." One of Chris's friends told him, early in the grief process, "You never get over the grief of losing your parents. It's gonna take time. It's gonna take time." Say it out loud with me: "It's gonna take time."

There is power in hearing others' stories about your loved one. Kate said, "I was touched by how many people were touched by my husband. I hadn't realized it." This realization was comforting. Leonard found that reaching out to others who had lost family members was illuminating: "Someone said—and this was helpful—that this would be like a wound, and there are times when it will open up again. It's true, and now that I've had more time to process it, I felt stuff I'd never felt before." Sometimes the wisdom of friends and family takes time to sink in.

Real Stories: The Power of Community

For many, being in community is crucial to survival in the early days of loss and grief. Chris affirmed the power of communal prayer: "You have to participate in the wake, the funeral, forty days. You're literally part of the body. You've lost a part of the body. Sometimes we don't know how to grieve together because we're afraid to love. We need to get together to just be." Francine felt that it "meant so much, the family, the church family, the ritual, the rules, physical things, the people. That's where the healing is."

Gabi is a self-described introvert and private person; she said, "I feel more comfortable grieving in silence, with myself." Her family's experience of grief was more outwardly directed. She said, "My aunts are very vocal, sharing memories, always talking and crying and laughing. That's what they needed."

Irene's father was a member of an Episcopal parish at the time of his sudden death. She remarked, "Even though [my dad] didn't have an Orthodox funeral, his church community did a Greek reception for us with coffee and Metaxa brandy, and these ladies looked up all these Greek food recipes on the Internet and made them. It was so touching." She and her family felt very supported.

Quinn experienced healing within her community. She said, "We had joyful sadness. I was happy [my departed friend] was with us all, all together, there were all the people she had helped, and so everybody was loving on her." Sasha noted, "The little ladies at my church, my dear friends, they were everything to me. [My friends] just showed up every Friday evening at my apartment, and they sat with me when I cried. Every week they did this. Eventually, they'd be like, let's take a walk. So, we'd do that. Little by little. They saved me. They were amazing."

Theo's mother was not Orthodox, and she had not wanted a funeral. "She wanted to be cremated, and she didn't want people to gather. We tried to respect her wishes, but we needed to mark her life, and to mark that event. It was more about her community. We were doing it, the memorial service, for us."

Theo and his family recognized that although his mother's beliefs did not prioritize a funeral, they needed to find a way to gather in community and mourn together.

CHAPTER NINE

Liturgical Grieving

Real Stories: The Funeral Rite

MY INTERVIEWEES SHARED emotional memories of the funeral. Anna said, "I never wanted [my husband's] funeral to end. It was the most beautiful liturgy I've ever been to." She added, "It gave me more time with him! We showed love and respect. I loved all of it. The sadness, the joy, the resurrectional tones. It felt like I could touch him emotionally and spiritually and physically. It was the best way to process. For me, it made sense."

Bonnie was thankful that her loved one's funeral was "a spiritual experience. Pow, it all hit me at the funeral." Chris felt strongly that "in the funeral, it's like God's walking with you. I began to listen to the words." Elena said, "It was very, very touching. It was uplifting. Honestly what uplifted me the most was all the flowers. It was so comforting!"

Francine felt that the liturgical cycle afforded her a meaningful framework to process her grief: "It's like birth and death: funeral, forty days, memorials." She is a member of her parish choir and an active reader, so for her, it felt "really good that the ritual was something I knew. It was so familiar and helpful. It was part of getting back to myself again. The funeral was like a period after a very long sentence" (five years of her mother's slow decline due to dementia).

Hazel said, "The moment I walked in, I broke down. But it was okay. It was very, very comforting. In our faith, there is no need, actually there is no place, for denial. You see it, you accept it, in the moment." As we discussed in Section One, our funerals provide a chance to face the real pain of death in the midst of the joy of the life-giving cross, tomb, and resurrection on the third day. Our funerals teach us how to grieve as fully as possible.

My participants who have little memory of the funeral still remember some moments of beauty. Leonard noted, "I don't remember a lot from the funeral, because I was in shock, I think. But I do remember our two priests chanting the evlogetaria in tone five, back and forth, back and forth, and it was unbelievably beautiful. My Jewish friends thought that was just so beautiful too." Nedim said, "I don't remember it, honestly. I don't remember the wake or the funeral. It was a blur." This related to his overall experience of stress and managing his family members and children after his wife's death.

Priscilla noted that our funeral, with its mix of sorrow and resurrectional joy, can be a bit confusing for the non-Orthodox. Her mother's funeral took place during Bright Week, so the clergy wore white vestments. "I warned my family members who aren't Orthodox . . . just so you know, at the funeral there's not going to be a lot of black, it's not going to be somber." And indeed, "All the vestments were white, and everything was bright, and they still all wore black and kind of stood in the corner awkwardly. They were all kind of like, 'What's going on?' It was so different from what they were used to!"

The liturgical gestures of the funeral were powerful for Kate's grief process: "The last kiss was so meaningful. I could see who all was there. I could greet them, really see their faces."

Leonard was not emotionally prepared for the funeral itself: "I had never seen a dead body before I saw my father at his funeral. I was twenty-three, but I was ill prepared because my family hadn't let me go to funerals in the past." As his parents had tried to protect him from grief, he was left unprepared when the time came for his father's funeral. We do well to note that even the most well-intentioned attempts at protection can have the effect of overwhelming a newly bereaved person, who is not prepared for the powerful experience of an Orthodox funeral.

Elena and her husband sang in the choir for their son's funeral. She said, "We do not grieve alone. We're never not singing. That's what we do." Mark noted, regarding his brother, "At the funeral, he looked weirdly serene. In a good way. Very peaceful, which was interesting because he'd had a difficult life." The funeral offered Mark a vision that he had not been afforded previously: his brother, fully at peace.

The burial gave Kate a strong sense of the seriousness of death and the hope of the resurrection. She remarked, "The burial was very somber. I wanted to wait all the way to the end, while they lowered the casket. Such a deep, deep silence. Then we all sang Pascha resurrection songs, and that lady who worked at the cemetery said she could have listened to that music forever!"

Mark also was struck with an intense feeling of solemnity: "There's something very real about seeing someone go into the ground. The nuns were singing 'Christ is Risen,' and some were crying too. It was a powerful juxtaposition. I saw a fox and a bunny jumping around in the grass near his grave. I liked the life around him." This was a vision of life and death, bunnies and foxes amidst the graves, people singing and crying together. Again, we see this deeply Orthodox way of navigating reality by holding seeming opposites together. This is what we mean by "joyful sorrow."

Priscilla was highly aware of the connection between her mother's funeral and our liturgical calendar. She said with a laugh, "My mother was a dancer, and she had great timing! To die during Holy Week, and to have her funeral on Bright Monday? Could that be more perfect? Basically, all we sang was 'Christ is Risen!' It was so joyful and bright. And now [the hymn] 'The Angel Cried' has so much depth to it!" Her joy was evident as she described the familiar "bright sadness" we profess as Orthodox Christians.

Quinn stated that the funeral directly helped her process of bereavement: "The funeral helped our grief. The funeral takes you through where you need to be. It's the meaning of life, in the first place. The story's not over." The Orthodox funeral gave the bereaved a chance to experience the loss—even seeing their loved one go into the ground—while singing and crying with the hope of the resurrection.

Real Stories: Memorials

The Church's practice of memorials is an important way for us to connect with and pray through our grief. Irene was comforted by the memorials for her parents as well as monthly memorials at her parish: "I'm a chanter at my church, so I was constantly chanting the memorials. It was three years before I could get through it without breaking down, but the other chanters would cover for me. I love doing the memorials. It's so comforting!" Anna actually wished for more memorials: "I really loved it all. I could have done a panakhida every day after [my husband's] death."

For Priscilla, "The forty-day memorial was really great. A lot of my friends and coworkers came, and we all could pray together. It's the church basically saying, you can start resuming normal life, if you want. It's like those forty days are protected." Hazel "liked the idea of forty days. Forty days off of everything. It made me so comforted even when I was so sad. I was so exhausted. It gave me time I needed." The forty-day memorial sets aside a block of time to grieve intensely, helps the bereaved visit the grief within the parish community, and provides a nudge back into daily life.

Several participants see memorials as a way to stay in touch with their grief. Sasha noted, "Every memorial, the grief comes back. I cry every time I'm at church." The memorials also support those whose loved ones were not church members. Theo said, "Even though my Mom wasn't Orthodox, I think of her whenever we pray for the dead. It provides a way to keep remembering those who have gone before us. I like that about the faith." Along these lines, Daria noted, "Even though [my dear friend] wasn't Orthodox, I always light a candle for him, and I think of him during the memorials."

Theo also feels this universality in memorials. He noted, "The memorials are for us all to witness. Even if we don't know the person. Even if it's someone's cousin in a different country. And while we're starting coffee hour here, maybe in California they're starting to pray. All around the world, there are memorials." The memorials facilitate grief by encouraging us to pray both for our specific loved ones and for the entire world.

Real Stories: Liturgical Life

Regular participation in liturgical life, both at home and in the parish, is a source of peace and comfort for many of us. It brings connection and helps to fight the isolation inherent in grief. Chris liked to "sit with Our Lady of Sorrows, the Theotokos icon. I sit with the icon of Christ as the Bridegroom. I heard the lamentations for Dormition and Pascha. That was so healing. I still had the grief to go through, but you don't have the sense of being alone." Bonnie noted, "In church, we call the angels in, and the angels protect us, and the saints pray along with us."

A few participants remarked that losing a loved one granted them a renewed and vibrant understanding of liturgy. Irene said, "We always hear about the liturgy on earth, and the liturgy of the angels in heaven. I never understood that until my parents died. But I know they are having liturgy right along with me." Jackie still "find[s] it immensely healing. During the Cherubic hymn, time just stops. I love it."

And when Priscilla is at church, she "think[s] about how my experience of God has widened, it's extended, to have someone that close to me who has fallen asleep in the Lord. It widens the circle." She and others noted that the depths of our emotion are contained in our liturgical life. Francine reminded me that "we don't need to fill [our liturgy] in with feelings. It just *is*. And that's enough!" Priscilla concurs: "Honestly, the best grief counseling was hearing the Paschal homily of St. John Chrysostom, the week that [my mother] died. Not one dead remains in the tomb, because Christ is risen!"

Real Stories: The Role of the Clergy

The priests of my participants were generally supportive in their grief. Leonard said, "The day [my dad] died, my priest told me—and I'll never forget this!—to read First Corinthians 15. In short, if Christ isn't raised from the dead, then our preaching is in vain, and our faith is in vain. That really affected me!" Leonard's priest also "walked [him] and [his] brother down the aisle to see [their] father. It was unbelievably kind."

Since the Orthodox funeral service is standardized in a way that many other funerals are not, there is often no liturgical opportunity to share details or feelings about the deceased. Leonard noted, "The priest said, 'I can't tell you about [Leonard's father] or his musical career, others will do that at the meal, but I can tell you about his faith in Jesus Christ and in the resurrection.'" At the other extreme, Quinn's priest encouraged personal storytelling: "Our priest asked people to share about [our friend] in the funeral. Right at the end, in the church. He comes from a Protestant background, so he wanted people to share."

Real Stories: Grieving a Miscarriage

Jackie shared how even well-intended actions can hurt a grieving person. Jackie and her husband have one young son, and she has had three heartbreaking miscarriages. She had a negative pastoral experience after one of the miscarriages: "My priest came up to me because he had heard I'd had yet another miscarriage. Without asking me, he said, 'We have to do this prayer, it may be hard to hear, but it will be helpful.' Then he launched into that old miscarriage prayer, the one that mentions murder and abortion, implying it is the mother's fault." She said, "I went to the choir loft and sobbed. I was broken by it. I can't tell you how angry I am. It took me almost a year to realize how much it hurt me."

The language of this prayer amplified Jackie's grief, compounding it with guilt and shame. She noted that her priest "kept telling me to think about the holiness of the Mother of God. He equated holiness with fertility." She likened this experience to one of Dr. Kubler-Ross's phases of grief: "Now I realize I was basically stuck in that bargaining phase of grief . . . like, 'If only I can do these prayers, be holier, more pure, I will earn God's favor.' He said [the miscarriages] could be from my unrepentant sin." She stated emphatically, "I want everyone to know that automatically using this prayer is not compassionate, and there are better prayers that can be used." This experience was profoundly hurtful to Jackie and her husband.

I share this story, painful as it is, to remind the reader that many Orthodox jurisdictions have a renewed understanding of the best way to minister to a mother and family grieving the loss of an unborn child. For example, the Holy Synod of

Bishops of the Orthodox Church in America revised the prayer in 2015, omitting the language about "murder" and "abortion," replacing it with healing language that honors the reality of loss and turns our hearts toward God:

> O Master, Lord our God, Who was born of the holy Theotokos and ever-Virgin Mary, and as a child was laid in a manger: In Thy great mercy be merciful to this, Thy handmaid [N.] who has miscarried the child who was conceived in her. Forgive all her voluntary or involuntary offenses, and protect her from all the machinations of the devil. Heal her suffering, and in Thy love for mankind grant health and strength to her body and soul. Guard her with a radiant Angel from every assault of the invisible demons and from every illness and malady, and deliver her from all that may afflict her womb. O Thou, Who accepts the innocence of infancy into Thy Kingdom, comfort the mind of Thy handmaid and bring her peace. Therefore, with fear we cry and say: Look down from heaven and strengthen Thy handmaid [N.] who has miscarried of the child conceived in her. Have mercy on her and bless her, through the intercession of Thine undefiled Mother and of all Thy Saints.[114]

Real Stories: On Grieving as an Orthodox Christian

Participants felt that the Orthodox faith helps us name our grief with boldness and open-heartedness. Chris, a convert from a Protestant denomination, said, "In other traditions, it's too open-ended. But we don't mince words! We don't edit anything! You say, hey Lord, this is what I'm struggling with."

Some noted a particular emphasis on prayerful conversation with the dead. Hazel said, "I always sort of talked to people in heaven before I became Orthodox, and now I realize that

Orthodox people do this. Conversing with the saints is acceptable!" Her instinct to pray and converse with saints was already part of Holy Tradition. Robel noted, "The prayers are so real, my mother was right there in the funeral, and everyone was wailing. She is with the saints now, we believe."

Further, we allow space for a sense of mystery. Nedim spoke of the limits of his comprehension without being troubled by them: "I don't know what heaven's like. I don't claim to know. But [my wife's belief in heaven] worked for her. It helped her manage the sorrow and horror of dying at a young age." Daria echoes this humility: "I try not to fill in the gaps. It's a mystery." Sasha, too, experienced grace along with humility: "God didn't answer our prayers, at least that's what I thought, but I also know [my loved one's] faith was so beautiful. And I've been taught humility."

Olga was grateful for God's presence through her grief and sees her faith as a blessing: "We are so blessed with the Orthodox faith. We know that God is with us." She has developed a clearer discernment of God's merciful love: "I prayed so hard for [my grandfather] not to die. But now I see that when you pray, sometimes God says yes, sometimes no, and sometimes, 'I have something better for you.' My faith is stronger now. I am less afraid, and I know God is with me." Sasha reflected on heaven, saying, "I believe, we believe, that no matter how beautiful our liturgy is, our music is, it doesn't compare to where I hope [he] is. He hasn't missed anything! If anything, we are the ones missing out!"

CHAPTER TEN

The Spiritual Experience of Grieving

Real Stories: Waiting for the Fog to Clear

IT IS NORMAL to experience changes and shifts in our faith in the wake of a death. Not all deaths are peaceful. Not all deaths come at the end of a long, full life. Many deaths just feel profoundly "wrong," as if they should not have happened yet. This can be particularly the case with a traumatic loss—for example, if your child dies or your loved one dies in a tragic accident. I want to note that these types of traumatic losses may create a state of bereavement that is uniquely devastating. You may feel completely isolated, but you do not have to suffer alone. I strongly recommend working with a trained clinical therapist who has experience with trauma, and connecting with others who have experienced a similar type of loss. My heart goes out to you.

This type of loss can lead to a crisis of faith wherein our relationship with God is tested. Leonard experienced a crisis of faith on the sudden death of his father:

> I found myself making a conscious choice: I can't change this. I need to accept it and move on. But I didn't know how to grieve!

Eventually, I realized it was a test of faith, and I said I would take time to grow in my faith. It was my faith that got me through this. That's really when I started going to church, and learning to chant, and really immersing myself in church life.

If you experience a crisis of faith, don't lose heart. It is completely normal and understandable to question your faith and your identity. It is completely normal to question why you are carrying this burden and to wonder where God is amid all this. Talk to your priest, and ask him and others to pray for you. Hopefully your friends and family will understand. Go to confession and share your struggles; trust in the sacramental life of the Church. Treat this like a wound that needs constant attention and steady healing. Pray for patience and gentleness, and please try not to abandon your faith altogether. God is with us. God is close to the brokenhearted.

If you feel God is far off or inaccessible, I offer you an image that might resonate. I used to work as a hospice chaplain in the San Francisco Bay area of California. As I drove each early morning to my hospice office, I would pass by one of the tallest mountains in the area. Most days, I could see it easily in the morning sun, magnificent and mighty, and it often looked different from one day to the next: snowy at times, always craggy, multicolored in the sun.

One morning as I drove through Concord, the infamous Bay Area fog had rolled in. To my shock, I could see nothing. The mountain seemed to be gone. The fog was so thick that I couldn't see a single one of its 3,849 majestic vertical feet. I was stunned.

Here is my point: the mountain was still there. It wasn't gone. I just couldn't see it for the time being. In the same way, even though we have times where we feel far away or discon-nected from God, God is never truly gone. Sometimes we can't discern His presence or feel His love; we can't be certain our prayers are being heard. But we should keep looking and lis-tening and praying. Keep saying the words of our Holy Tradi-tion. Keep showing up and keep the eyes of your heart open, with patience and perseverance. God is always here, and the mountain is always there. Try to wait for the fog to roll out. Be patient with yourself, and God will still be there to love you.

Many of my participants shared reflections on newfound wisdom and growth after loss. Remember, this growth was not instantaneous; it took patience, trust, and an effort to process the emotions and challenges of grief. Sasha noted, "I can well and truly say possessions mean nothing to me, now that I've lost the most precious person in my life."

Mark also experienced a shift in his outlook on faith after his brother died: "Being the apophatic type, it's hard for me to name how it changed my faith. It's an all-encompassing thing. A few words that come to mind are clarity, less B.S. Basically, at that time I had the most profound losses I could imagine, my brother and my professional career as I knew it. An existential Band-aid was ripped off. But I made it through. I've survived the two things I most didn't want, and I now feel immune to most of life's darts as a result. I'm less afraid of hardship, and I am better at forgiveness. I had to forgive him. Also, other words that come to mind are infinity, and veils. Like veils of awareness."

Bonnie said, "The Lord has always been a comfort. My rela-tionship with Him has grown. The Lord is working whether people want Him to or not." Irene also experienced growth in the face of grief: "It deepened my faith. And the loss deepened my sense of the limitations of being human, and the love of God, the overseeing of God. It helped me see the previous limits of my faith, and that actually we are swimming in an ocean of God! Everything is from God. Everything!" She is mindful of her own death: "I remember the finite nature of my own life, and I think about meeting God at my death. I'm approaching the 'no green bananas' stage.* I want to be prepared."

Jackie noted, "I finally understand incredible joy and incredible sorrow. I've lived it. God is with us in that." Nedim said, "[My wife's death] improved my Christian practice. I had tried to be kind and generous. But that's more established now. My wife was a truly kind and giving person. I think I've taken on some of my wife's character, like a merger that's happening or is complete." This process of growth takes time, patience, and attentiveness to the ways that God is present with us in grief.

Real Stories: Why We Need an Orthodox Bereavement Group

Two of my participants had a negative experience in a community bereavement group. They specifically attributed this to the group's secular foundations. Hazel said, "The regular bereavement group was a little too woo-woo for me. It was like [the group leaders] were trying too hard, including all the religions. Including atheists. Which is just different from what we believe." Gabi said, "I did not like the support group. Everyone believed different things and were there to vent, with nothing to

---

* Meaning, there may be no time left for bananas to ripen.

hold them up. It wasn't comforting. It was depressing." Though Gabi had a foundation of faith, attending the group was disorienting.

Most of my participants did not attend a community-based group because they didn't need or want secular support. Bonnie noted, "It's hard for me to relate to people who don't have faith as a focal point." Hazel, too, said, "I don't know how people who aren't believers get through."

Olga's faith radiated through her statement about the uniqueness of Orthodoxy: "The thing is, the Orthodox believe differently than a lot of people. My friend at work lost his son, and he just keeps saying, 'I don't believe in God now, what kind of a God would do this to me?' But I just have to say to him, 'We don't understand this, it's a mystery, and we live in a fallen world.' Jesus came, Jesus Himself died to abolish death, we are healed in death." She went on to say, "Imagine if we were here, and Jesus never came? I can't imagine!" She has tried to share a compassionate understanding with her grieving coworker, but without the broader context, it can be hard to connect in a meaningful way.

Fifteen out of twenty participants said they would attend an Orthodox bereavement group if one were available in their area. One said she would not attend such a group because she is an introvert and preferred to process her grief privately. The other four said "maybe." A few elaborated on the "maybe" answers. For instance, Mark said, "I would go to a group if there were no intense doctrinal pressures, a thoughtful blending of theory sharing and emotional expression. And confidentiality." Kate echoed this interest in staying away from strict doctrine or rigid sensibilities, saying, "I would love a group that is Orthodox as long as it isn't stuck in doctrine. I need to have a place to feel bad. I don't want just to hear, 'Don't be sad because he is with the saints.' I need a mix of sorrow and gladness. I think that is pretty Orthodox, honestly. You know, joyful sorrow."

Theo said, "I would feel way more comfortable going to an Orthodox group. I don't think there's anything like that. Coffee hour is tough. It's hard to move from surface friendships and conversations to deeper friendships. It's not enough." Mark noted, "I'd like a group where you can weep and show the physiology of emotional experience without normal containment." In other words, it is important for an Orthodox bereavement group to have a strong theological foundation that allows for confidentiality, flexibility, honesty, and a variety of genuine emotional expression.

Quinn summarized her belief that Orthodox theology facilitates a dynamic understanding of grief: "In a lot of Protestant funerals, they make the assumption that you are going to heaven. Going 'home.' Which is good, of course. But there's something wrong with this, to me. You don't really get to grieve. And there's something deeper going on that gets shoved aside. There's some loss of understanding of death and resurrection. And that's all there [in the Orthodox faith]. Deep theology! The sacraments are really amazing! If you listen and pay attention, you will learn something. You gotta be working on that! Pay attention! Pray for this person. We pray for the dead. I don't know what really goes on, but the idea is you need to keep praying for them. I mean, what can you do for them? You pray for them."

Real Stories: Christ Is Risen!

I believe Anna summarized it best when she said, "My friend wore all white to her husband's funeral, and when everyone kept saying, 'I'm sorry, I'm sorry,' she replied over and over with 'Christ is Risen!' That's all you can say, all you need to say. So that's what I did when [my husband] died. I wore a white dress, and I said 'Christ is risen!'"

Truly, that is all we collectively need to say. I hope these stories have made it clear that our faith reaches into the depths of grief, and our liturgical practices help us experience the many facets of loss. Our faith allows for a full expression of loss, including joy, sorrow, silence, connection, and peace. Both personally and communally, the faith teaches us how to nourish a grieving heart and how to grow as Christians in the midst of joyful sorrow.

CHAPTER ELEVEN

Nurturing Our Connections

Real Stories: Ongoing Connection to Loved Ones

D O YOU FEEL as if you have an ongoing connection with your loved one? Do you associate him or her with something: a bird, a butterfly, a song, a rainbow? Most of my interviewees still feel connected to their loved ones, and they experienced this connection in many ways. Bonnie felt "like the Holy Spirit was sending [her] connections." Chris said of his deceased parents, "I have sensed their presence. After my recent surgery, they were with me. Just enough of a glimpse of them."

I associate my Grandma Byrne with butterflies. After I attended her funeral, I took home a small fabric monarch butterfly that decorated one of the many flower arrangements. I began seeing monarchs in unexpected places: along a highway in the middle of nowhere, outside a Chinese restaurant, here and there. I checked a book out of the divinity school library shortly after her funeral, and someone had stuck a printed color photo in the book with a beautiful image of—you guessed it—a monarch butterfly. At my bridal shower, many of my grandmother's daughters, nieces, and granddaughters stood around chatting.

We started talking and reminiscing about Gram, and wouldn't you know it, we looked up and—surprise!—there was a beautiful monarch circling above us. What a blessing! Whatever it means, those small moments remind me of her, and I cherish them.

Daria echoed this: "It's all absolutely connected. I take comfort knowing that somehow, they are out there. Is it because I'm thinking of them, or is it the fact that we don't have words for it? I don't know." She is comfortable with that mystery and sees it as part of life as an Orthodox Christian. Kate feels "absolutely connected. Since he died, my journals have been letters to him. Dear [husband], I'm sick of you being dead. Enough already! Where did you go?" She laughed as she shared this, expressing joy and sadness.

Francine related that not only does she feel connected to her mother, but their relationship continues to evolve and expand. She feels that our loved ones are "alive in our memory and in our lives." Her relationship with her mother was complicated; it was not always pleasant or positive. She said, "In a selfish way, I'm still trying to work out my relationship with her. Every now and then, I have a sense of her person. Forget the craziness, I feel her, and that she's here and alive. The good lives on, her essence." The complex relationship made her grief harder, in a certain sense: "My grief was tied into the finality of not figuring out our relationship, not quite fixing everything. But I came to see the good side of her." She continues to grow into a more peaceful relationship with her mother. She smiled as she shared this.

Hazel "certainly feels [her husband] is alive." And yet she notes, "But I wish he was here, with me. I have asked him to pray for me in heaven." Irene shared how she emptied out her loved one's home and moved some cherished furniture into her own home. After doing this, she said, "One night, I knew he was here. I spoke to him: 'If I see you, it will terrify me. But I love you, and I'm glad you're here.'" She often says at night, to her parents, "I love you and I miss you. Their abiding presence is wonderful, but not to speak to them, to hold them, is so hard." She cried as she shared this reminder that love, hope, and heartbreak are intertwined for those who grieve.

The topic of connection through dreams was raised frequently. Anna shared, "I kept thinking I would have more dreams about him. But I mostly feel him. Like we have a background dialogue all the time." Bonnie's sister had "many dreams" about their father, though she personally did not. She feels strongly that "the Lord used my dad's death, my faith, and my sister's dreams to bring us all together" as a family. Kate had "several dreams, two where I woke up and then I was glad [my husband] was dead because the dreams were confusing and sad. That sounds weird. But I mean, he was suffering, and I know he is with God. This earth really isn't the best place to be, you know."

Leonard conveyed that his ongoing relationship with his late father is a profound source of revelation and joy. He noted, "I have so many incredible examples of my dad reaching out to us since his death. He was a multi-instrumentalist and played with a ton of musicians in the seventies and eighties. To me, his voice wasn't his speaking voice. It was his oboe, his English horn, his clarinet. Any time I hear him on the radio, it's like he is speaking to me. For example, on the day of his death, we had a long drive back home to prepare for the funeral. And bingo, in the car on the radio, there was his English horn solo on [a world-famous pop singer's] song. It was like he was with us!"

Leonard believes his father reached out to him, accompanying him with his musical "voice," on the grief-stricken drive home for the funeral. He feels that his father has kept reaching out over the years: "Many years later, when my brother and his wife found out they were having a baby, a son, they walked into the receptionist's office and immediately the song came on! It was like my dad was present with them and aware of the fact that my brother was becoming a dad to a son. It was amazing."

Olga shared stories of ongoing and dynamic connections with loved ones: "I have a very strong presence of my grandfather. Also my aunt; when I'm half-asleep, it's almost like a vision, hopefully you don't think this is crazy, but I get these visions! My aunt who died would always joke with us, and one time I saw her in this vision, and she was with my grandmother who died, their arms were linked. My aunt said, 'We're all here! We'll all be together again.' And then, of course, because she always joked, she said, 'Not too soon though. And this one [gesturing to my grandmother], all she does is watch, watch, watch.'"

Olga believes "they watch over us, and pray for us. What a blessing! With my grandfather, sometimes I know he is present, and I'll say, I know you're here, and I love you." Olga shared powerful stories of the continuing bond with her grandfather.

One such occurrence happened years ago, when her children were teenagers and she had recently gone through an unusually stressful period. One evening, she had chest pains and thought she was having a heart attack. She called the ambulance, and as they were driving away, the paramedic asked who else was in the house: "Just the two children and the older gentleman, right?" Olga responded that the only other people who lived there were her two children. The paramedic was confused. "When we picked you up, there was that older gentleman there, behind you?" Olga believes that her grandfather "revealed himself when [she] was in danger." She feels that "the paramedic saw him somehow. It's insane! How could she have seen that? She described him. Honestly, it's good that I didn't see him, because I probably would have died from that heart attack!"

Quinn shared that her connection to her friend has actually grown: "I feel closer to her than ever because she's not bound by her body. You're thinking and worshipping all the time in the presence of the saints, we have relics too, we as Orthodox, so it's not that far-fetched. It's not a woo-woo, contacting the spirits stuff, because the world is reasonably more than just contact with our senses. You stand in the presence of the saints. I talk to her, she was a real struggler, she probably still is. Since she passed, we feel her. I can see her blessings."

Quinn feels particularly connected to her friend at the graveside. She said, "At our farm, we have an old cemetery. Established in 1872. Slaves, paupers, and Indians, that's what the sign says. God's people. We had the cemetery consecrated, and [my friend] is buried there. She is with us. I don't have visitations or hear her voice, but I'm assured of her presence."

Real Stories: When a Relationship Is Complicated

Some people do not feel they have an ongoing relationship with the deceased. This may be the case for you, and it is perfectly normal. You may have had a traumatic relationship that causes you pain, and it's okay to be honest about this (and I hope you can address this with a trained therapist).

For example, Mark had a complicated relationship with his brother. When asked if he has an ongoing connection with his brother, he said, "Mostly not, because it would have negative psychological consequences, because of [our painful history]. I focused on saying goodbye to him. I still pray for him and have visions of him, mystical ones."

This is important to note: all the participants, whether or not they have ongoing connections, pray for their loved ones. They do this simply, without anger or judgment. As Mark noted further, "My gut says we are connected. My mid-level understanding thinks it may not be real. But my higher understanding, my mystical side, thinks of course we are still connected," and hence he prays for his brother.

Reflecting on the relationship with his deceased wife, Nedim said, "I dream of her occasionally, but I don't think our relationship is ongoing exactly, instead that she has moved on and is settled wherever she went." Her moving on does not reflect a difficult or fraught relationship; rather, it's indicative of peace and rest. He noted, "In the culture I grew up in, if you feel someone's presence, messing with you, that means they are not at peace. I don't feel that way about my wife. She's at peace, wherever she is. Like my grandma, when she shows up, it's not good. She messed with us all the time!"

Theo had a complex relationship with his mother, and he does not feel they have an ongoing relationship. He said, "I don't hear her voice, although I know some people do hear the voice of someone who died, like my friend's brother always sends her signs, or guidance, funny coincidences, that kind of thing." He feels that in some ways he had to let go of her, and more specifically his painful relationship with her, for the last years of her life. They were "not close toward the end. If anything, I feel connected to the way she raised me. What she gave us, what she sacrificed. I am who I am because of that. So I guess that's the connection that's ongoing." Theo's sense of himself, of surviving and thriving through adversity, is connected to his mother's care for him. In this sense they are connected, and he remembers her in prayer.

A fraught relationship does not prevent Elena from having an ongoing connection. Elena's son died after many painful years of struggle with addiction and mental health. She said, "I go through phases: I miss him, I'm angry, I feel his presence, a sense of him. In some ways, I feel more in relationship with him since he died. I've had dreams where there is such joy. One dream, he said 'I'm going to a wedding.' I loved that!" She maintains a certain prayerful and peaceful stance toward her son, with compassion, knowing that he suffered greatly in his earthly life and he is now in a place of rest.

Real Stories: The Meaning of Memory Eternal

My interviewees' interpretation of the phrase "memory eternal" was rich and varied. Some people interpret it to mean that our loved ones are alive through Christ. One aspect of "memory eternal" is the idea that our loved ones continue to live within our memories. Anna felt that "God willing, in my opinion, my husband is on his way to being with the saints. He is part of a big living family. It's the body of saints, held in our hearts.

We are connected." Bonnie felt the phrase means that "since [her] father died in Christ, then he's with us." Chris said, "It's a mystery. [My mother] remains both in the body of Christ and on that greater shore of those who stood before the throne of God." Saying "memory eternal" brings profound comfort to Elena; she noted, "I really experience [my son] alive. I feel his joy. I know that he is alive in Christ."

Daria was taught that "memory eternal" means "that you need to remember your relatives, and they can intercede for you." Francine echoes this sense of family connection: "Saying 'memory eternal' is a way to make sure I remember her, to keep her real in my mind, in my memory." Gabi noted that her father "lives on in our memories. The feeling I have is that he left this world feeling comfortable that I was comfortable. He had nothing to worry about. He left in peace." Irene boldly stated, "It means [my loved one] never died at all. We don't die; we go on. It's the hope that there is someone to remember you."

To Kate, "memory eternal" means "[my husband] has a lot of people praying for him. Each soul is from God and always of God. Not just being remembered on earth, but a long line of beings who are connected to God." Leonard knows his father "is still present in [his] life. He is in heaven and we never forget about him; he's there with us in the Liturgy, he interacts with me."

In addition, participants shared that "memory eternal" is not only about our human memory, but also God's memory of us. Irene shared, "Whether there is someone to remember you here or not, the person is always remembered by God." This resonated with Francine as well: "You are living in God's memory, in eternal life." Daria noted, "To me, it's not just your relatives, it really reflects God's immortal time. It's the bigger picture. Eternal. That word is very powerful!"

For Quinn the phrase evokes a profound distillation of grief, death, and hope: "When the nun sang 'Memory Eternal' at my friend's funeral, that was it. That was all I needed to hear! The end. Perfect." As Quinn noted, "Not too long ago I found out it's not just that you remember someone, but are remembered by God. In remembering, we remember death, and we remember that God loves us, He always loves us. I love the person I'm singing for, and if I don't particularly know the person, then it's about how God loves us."

Some participants noted that "memory eternal" is not easily definable. Jackie said, "It's kind of confusing. The grammar in English is a bit vague, there's probably some Greek thing I'm missing! The way I see it, I'm asking for the strength to remember the person who passed. Maybe it also means to be remembered in heaven, and asking God to give me the grace to remember what a blessing this person was."

Mark reflected on the richness of the phrase, in a quote worth sharing in its entirety: "It's so interesting. Is it 'memory eternal' for me, humanity, the world, souls, or is it God's memory, a process? It's not like I'm producing memory eternal. It's not in the past. More like perception eternal. Like in God's time, God's 'now.' It's almost just a word for us. If everything is present to God, God doesn't need a memory. It's for the community. It's more than knowing a person has existed. It's memory toward present perception of life in God." Mark's statement reflects the dynamic relationship between present time and eternity.

Theo echoed this concept when he said, "It means keeping

that person's life, their existence, in mind. It can be easy to forget people. And when our time comes, we will remain in their memory. It's a way to look forward and backward together, as a community." As we look forward and backward, we join together within the present moment of prayer and remembrance.

Echoing this dynamic, Sasha noted, "By praying [memory eternal], does that mean [he] will be in Paradise? I don't know. Let's say, I remember my grandparents. My nephew and niece will remember me. But who is going to remember three generations more?" Sasha continued, "It's not eternal if it's limited to our life time. No, I guess I take it to mean that I will remember [him] at the memorials, and I also know that matters of this world are temporary. So what then? God remembers!"

Real Stories: Summary

Most of the Orthodox Christians I spoke with had a sense of ongoing connection with their loved ones. This includes hearing their voices, seeing them in dreams, or having a general sense of their presence. Those participants who did not have a strong sense of ongoing connection had different reasons for this. Some simply feel their loved one is at rest. For others, the painful or complex nature of their relationship does not inspire ongoing connection. However, every one of my participants noted that they pray for their loved one. The commitment to praying for them, and the belief that they pray for us, is powerful and enduring. I encourage you to adopt the practice of praying for your loved ones and asking them to intercede for us.

Reflecting on the concept of "memory eternal" is fruitful. Though we utter this prayerful phrase over and over, at every funeral and every memorial, there is not one unified interpretation. Instead, reflecting on its meaning gives rise to contemplation of our human memory, our participation in the body of Christ, and our sense of God's omniscient connection to His people. We are blessed with a powerful gift of memory and prayer within the body of the Church. Regardless of the type or nature of the relationship, we believe that our prayers are meaningful and bring peace at a time of grief. To say "memory eternal" is both deeply personal, when we name our own loved ones, and deeply universal, in that we still pray together even if we never met the person we commemorate. In remembering those who have gone before us, we remember death, and we remember that God loves us, in His eternal memory.

Notably, as I reflect on the stories of grieving Orthodox people, there is no obvious difference between converts and those born into Orthodoxy in the quality or attitudes toward grief. Neither was there a discernible difference in belief among those of different ethnic backgrounds or jurisdictions, though specific practices around food and other local traditions varied. Whether they had an Orthodox or a non-Orthodox loved one, the core of the bereaved person's grief response was the practice of faith. It was both the primary place (the parish) and primary framework for understanding death and life. For those with a non-Orthodox loved one, the lack of an Orthodox funeral sometimes made it harder to have a liturgical way to process the loss. Thankfully, for these people, the subsequent experience of memorials at their own parish was meaningful and healing.

Grief is both universal and personal, individual and communal. It can be spoken and silent; it can offer us tears of sorrow and tears of joy. Remember in quiet times of sorrow to take a moment to listen at the heart level to God's voice and God's love. Be still and listen. Christ never promised us that every single one of our prayers will get answered exactly the way we want. But He promised us something even better: that He is always with us. God will never abandon us, for "He Himself has said: 'I will never leave you nor forsake you'" (Heb. 13:5).

Sometimes the presence of God is not dramatic—we are not always knocked to the ground by it as was St. Paul. Instead, sometimes God's love emerges out of humble silence. Recall how in 1 Kings, God instructs Elijah to stand on the mountain. God sends a mighty wind that breaks the rocks in pieces, but God is not in the wind. He sends an earthquake and a fire, but God's voice is not within them. Finally, God speaks to Elijah in a still and small voice. The Hebrew phrase is *kol d'mama dakah*—literally, "the voice of a thin silence."

This voice of God's presence is there for us in our grief, our sorrow, and our stories. Whether we are joyfully singing and chanting at church or sitting in quiet prayer and contemplation, we are honoring our grief.

The Memory Eternal Bereavement Group Guide

Overview of the Guide

THE MEMORY ETERNAL Bereavement Group Guide is an eight-week program intended to help you to explore your grief from an Orthodox Christian perspective, to connect and pray with others, and to experience renewal and hope. The goal of this guide is not to get over grief or somehow complete a journey of grief. Honestly, most grievers I know dislike the term "journey." It implies a beginning and an end. Instead, perhaps we can think of this process as a grief rollercoaster (that eventually becomes less bumpy) or a contemplative grief labyrinth. (A labyrinth is not to be confused with a maze. In mazes, you can get lost. In labyrinths, you trust the path, though it is circuitous, and you cannot get lost.)

The goal of this program is to find ways to live with grief. The goal is to talk and think through the pain of grief, share memories, and learn to live with joy, while knowing you are forever changed. The goal is to draw on our deep, rich heritage as Orthodox Christians—to explore the prayers of the Church and the Scriptures, which teach us how to live in bright sadness.

The curriculum is designed to be used with others—for example, as a parish-based bereavement group. However, some readers may prefer to process grief more privately. If you are one of these, I encourage you to use the curriculum for personal guidance, for weekly conversations with a friend, for journaling, or however you see fit. If you are interested in using this guide as a bereavement group curriculum, please see the Facilitator's Guide in Appendix I before starting the group.

Giving Yourself Time and Space to Grieve

In the Orthodox Church, the traditional saying after a loved one dies is, "May his/her memory be eternal." Remembering is not just thinking of the person you love in some abstract way. "Re-membering" is keeping him or her as a member of your family, a member of your community, a member in your heart. We remain in communion with the departed in the body of Christ. We profess that Christ has trampled down death by death, and upon those who are in the tombs, He has bestowed life. Those who have died are alive in Christ! We proclaim a faith that regards the cross of Christ with both sorrow and joy, and we find peace in God's love for all His people. We honor the loss of your loved one, and we grieve with hope.

To remember is to sing your father's favorite song to your kids at bedtime, to make your mother's classic recipe for peach cobbler or baklava, to retell those one-liners your husband used to say. To remember is to devote yourself to a cause that your best friend cared deeply about. To remember is to live in the way of your loved one, knowing you are forever changed. As we tell the stories of those we love—while crying, or laughing, or sometimes awkwardly doing both at the same time—we keep them close.

When we experience the death of a loved one, we grieve.

We feel lonely and isolated. We feel overwhelmed by details to remember, or we feel stuck and frozen in our shock. We might feel crazy or forgetful or numb. We feel fine one day, but the next day is unbearable. Friends and family may say helpful things, and even well-intentioned people may say things that hurt.

Grief changes our relationships and affects our families and friends. You may question who you are: will others still see you as a mother, as a wife, as a husband? Some people may avoid you; some of your relationships will change. Some friends will truly show up, and some may avoid you for a time.

We grieve loss in our bodies, minds, and spirits. Maybe you didn't expect grief to be so very physical. Sometimes you feel as if you can't breathe or you are stuck. I commend you for seeking out a place of fellowship where you may process your experience, share your emotions, and remember that God is present with us through grief. You don't have to do this alone.

The Orthodox liturgical tradition offers powerful communal practices, such as funerals and memorials, with prayers for the departed. Our tradition teaches us to grieve in prayer; we grieve in church, and we grieve together. Our prayers are richly healing and encourage us to see that Christ knows our suffering, that we are not alone, and that we should pray for our loved ones, just as they continue to pray for us.

Maybe your loved one was Orthodox Christian, and he or she had an Orthodox funeral. Maybe he or she was not Orthodox and did not have a funeral, or had a memorial service in another spiritual tradition. In either case, your grief is your own, and we encourage you to draw on your faith to seek comfort and peace. As we will explore in the guide, Orthodox Christians celebrate memorials for our deceased loved ones at the third day after the death, along with the ninth day, the fortieth day, and then annually. Even if your loved one was not Orthodox, these memorials are one way to remember him or her within the beautiful prayers of our faith community. We encourage you to name your loved one during the memorials at your parish.

Grief continues after the church services are over; for many, it lasts months and years, and for others, a lifetime. Due to the increasingly isolated society we live in, much of this grieving is unseen and private. Grief can create a quiet suffering that is not generally part of everyday conversation. As John O'Donohue writes, "When you lose someone you love, your life becomes strange. The ground beneath you gets fragile. Your heart has grown heavy with loss."[115] Does this resonate with you? As Christians, we must try our best to share the heaviness and fragility of loss with others, with love and compassion.

The Memory Eternal curriculum will provide you a space to grieve, to cry, and to lament. We do not assign time limits to grief; instead we frame grief through a lens of sorrowful joy and honor our loved ones in our eternal, connected memories. I invite you to participate in this curriculum with openness, love, and gentleness.

We will emphasize our framework of life-giving faith along with concepts such as continuing bonds—a secular grief concept that dovetails richly with the concept of memory eternal. The continuing bonds that exist among our loved ones provide a rich way to process loss. Again, we do not have to get over our loss! Instead, we may find a new, prayerful way to locate our loved one in our hearts and lives.

As we explore our experiences of grief, we may likely have unexpected moments of pain and sorrow. We may also, God willing, discover joyful moments of the peace that surpasses understanding. In the setting of Christian fellowship, we may share, connect, and heal through Christ who is ever present with us, both here on earth and in the Kingdom of heaven. Christ is Risen!

The Bereavement Group Guide

Week 1: Lamenting Your Loss
Grief Activity: Letter to Self

Week 2: Healing Found in Prayer and Liturgy
Grief Activity: Pray Every Day

Week 3: Your Community
Grief Activity: Reach Out to a Friend

Week 4: Memory Eternal
Grief Activity: Remembrance Box

Week 5: Continuing Bonds
Grief Activity: Letter to Your Loved One

Week 6: Forgiveness, Anger, and Self-Care
Grief Activity: Writing a Self-Care Plan

Week 7: How Grief Can Challenge Our Faith
Grief Activity: An Act of Kindness

Week 8: Bright Sadness
Grief Activity: Say Their Names

Lamenting Your Loss

Meeting Agenda

OPENING: TRISAGION PRAYERS

WELCOME AND INTRODUCTIONS

GROUP COVENANT

To be read aloud by leader and acknowledged by all group participants.

» All information in this group is private and confidential and will not be shared.

» Our meetings will begin and end on time. Please be punctual, and please silence your cell phone.

» Please make every effort to attend all sessions.

» Each person's grief is unique, so try to honor everyone's struggle and validate what they are going through.

» Refrain from offering advice, engaging in side conversations, interrupting others, or making judgments.

» Allow time for others to speak, being mindful not to monopolize the conversation, and allow for moments of silence.

» Be respectful and compassionate to other participants.

» Try not to compare your story of loss with others. All losses are challenging.

» Expressions of honest feelings are welcome, including but not limited to crying, anger, guilt, fear, and shame.

» Everyone will have an opportunity to share their story, and you may remain silent if you prefer. This is your group, and we welcome your ideas.

GOSPEL READING: MATTHEW 28:16–20

Stand together and choose one participant to read the Gospel aloud.

QUESTIONS FOR DISCUSSION

Each member should have the opportunity to answer the following questions.

1. Please tell the group about your loved one who has died. If you are comfortable, share the circumstances of the death and your current coping. Share a picture if you have one.

2. Everyone has different reactions to grief—some immediate, some delayed. Your reactions may be different from those of family members or friends. What are your emotional reactions like? Were you surprised by your responses? How have your emotions changed over time? When you were growing up, were you encouraged to express your emotions?

EXERCISE

Lauren Herschel offers us an image of grief as "a ball and a box." Picture a box with a ball and a red button inside it. That's the pain button. In the early days of grief, the ball is giant—it almost fills up the box. It's impossible to move the box without the ball rolling around and smacking the pain button. With every move you make, the ball hits the pain button, over and over, relentlessly. The pain is constant. Every aspect of your life hits the button: driving by your old favorite restaurant, seeing your loved one's coffee cup, picking up shirts at the dry cleaner, making cookies, doing a crossword puzzle, driving to church. Over time, the box stays the same size, but the ball gets smaller and hits the button less often. However, when it hits, it's just as painful as ever. It's also unpredictable, hitting the button three times in one day or giving you a week without pain. Living with grief is like this. Thankfully, the ball becomes smaller over time, but the pain of grief still surprises you, often coming out of nowhere.

Discuss this model of grief. Does it resonate with you? Could you picture your grief like this? Is this model helpful? Do you have other images for your grief process?

CLOSING: PRAYER OF THE HOURS

Read the prayer together.

At every time and at every hour in heaven and on earth You are worshipped and glorified, O Christ our God, You who are long-suffering, most merciful, most compassionate, who love the just and are merciful to sinners, who call all to salvation through the promise of the good things to come. Accept, O Lord, our entreaties at this hour and guide our lives that we may keep Your commandments. Sanctify our souls, purify our bodies, correct our thoughts, purify our ideas, and deliver us from all distress, evil, and pain. Surround us with Your holy angels that, protected and guided by their host, we may attain unity of faith and the knowledge of Your unapproachable glory. For blessed are You forever and ever. Amen.[116]

On Your Own

GRIEF ACTIVITY: LETTER TO SELF

Between Weeks One and Two, I invite you to write a letter to yourself in a journal. This is not for sharing with anyone (unless, of course, you want to). This letter is meant to encourage you to reflect on what you need, to acknowledge temptations or challenges, and to remind yourself that you are loved and cared for. Your letter does not have to be fancy or well written. It just needs to be bold and honest. Step outside yourself for a moment and give yourself a bit of compassion and care. Your letter might look something like this:

Dear Sarah,

Please remember to:

» Get at least eight hours of sleep each night.
» Not judge yourself for feeling sad and unmotivated.
» Not take other people's actions or comments personally. It's probably not about you.
» Put your face in the sun every day (be like a sunflower!).
» Have a good cry when you need it (and remember that if you feel emotionally stuck, you can watch the beginning

of *Up* or the end of *Big Fish*. They always make you cry.)
» Make yourself cozy with lots of blankets.
» Have fun and play outside with Rafael (your adorable child).
» Not worry about all the Legos and Pokémon cards on the floor or the clean laundry in the baskets. At least the laundry is clean!
» Have dance parties to '90s hip-hop with Rafa and Peter.
» Limit coffee to two cups a day.
» Drink a lot of water.
» Play and sing musical theater loudly in the car.
» Trust that you are growing and changing for the good.
» Eat vegetables every day.
» Stop mindlessly scrolling on social media.
» Read your favorite poetry.
» Go for a walk as often as possible.
» Notice small beautiful things in nature.
» Buy fresh flowers for yourself every week.
» Light a candle in the evenings and make yourself a hot beverage.
» Pray every day, and if you can't get all the words out, then just pray, "Lord, have mercy."

With love,
Sarah

Grief Wisdom for Week One

FROM SCRIPTURE

Now may the God of hope fill you with all joy and peace in believing, that you may abound in hope by the power of the Holy Spirit. (Rom. 15:13)

FROM LITURGY

O Death, where is your sting? O Hell, where is your victory? Christ is risen, and you are overthrown. Christ is risen, and the demons are fallen. Christ is risen, and the angels rejoice. Christ is risen, and life reigns. Christ is risen, and not one dead remains in the grave. For Christ, being risen from the dead, is become the first fruits of those who have fallen asleep. To Him be glory and dominion unto ages of ages. Amen. (Paschal Homily of St. John Chrysostom)[117]

FROM THE SAINTS

Stand at the brink of despair, and when you see that you cannot bear it anymore, draw back and have a cup of tea. (St. Silouan of Mount Athos)[118]

FROM CULTURE/LITERATURE

Poetically translated to "golden joinery," Kintsugi is the centuries-old Japanese art of fixing broken pottery. Rather than rejoining the broken pieces with a hidden adhesive, this technique employs a special lacquer dusted with powdered gold. Once completed, seams of gold glint in the conspicuous cracks of pottery, giving a one-of-a-kind appearance to each "repaired" piece. This method celebrates each artifact's history by emphasizing its fractures and breaks, instead of hiding or disguising them. In fact, this practice often makes the repaired piece even more beautiful than the original, revitalizing it with a new look and giving it a second life. When we lose someone, we see cracks in everything. The world as we knew it is broken. Invisibly gluing it back together the way it was is not possible. Yet maybe we can slowly fill the cracks. We can fill the cracks with love from others, with good memories, with belly laughs and real talk about blessings and struggles. Maybe we can highlight with gold those places that have changed, claiming them as our own, as beautiful even. With pottery, the gold is added at the end of the repair process, not at the initial point of brokenness. There is a great deal of work that must be done to repair the breaks before the gold is introduced. So it is with us. Healing comes by going through the work of grief, not by trying to disguise it.[119]

FROM A GRIEVING ORTHODOX CHRISTIAN

Sasha: The little ladies at my church, my dear friends, they were everything to me. My friends just showed up every Friday evening at my apartment, and they sat with me when I cried. Every week they did this. Eventually, they'd be like, "Let's take a walk." So we'd do that. Little by little. They saved me. They were amazing.

Healing Found in Prayer and Liturgy

Meeting Agenda
OPENING: TRISAGION PRAYERS

GROUP CHECK-IN
How are you coping this week?

GOSPEL READING: MARK 16:1–8
Stand together and choose one participant to read the Gospel aloud.

QUESTIONS FOR DISCUSSION
1. What was your loved one's funeral like? Did he or she have an Orthodox funeral? If not, what was the service like? What was comforting? What was most difficult? What surprised you? Some people have little memory of the funeral or the immediate time after a loved one's death. How much do you remember?

2. Were you able to go to funerals as a young person or were you kept at home? Did your family talk about grief and death? How has this affected you?

EXERCISE

Share one specific story about your loved one that makes you laugh.

CLOSING: PRAYER OF THE HOURS

Stand and read the prayer together (see Week One).

On Your Own

GRIEF ACTIVITY: PRAY EVERY DAY

Between Weeks Two and Three, I would like to lovingly challenge you to step up your prayer life. If you already have a prayer rule, great job! Keep it up and consider adding a new prayer or daily Scripture reading. If you do not already have a personal rule of prayer, try praying the morning and/or evening prayers of the Church. You could pray the beautiful Morning Prayer of St. Philaret of Moscow:

> O Lord, grant me to greet the coming day in peace. Help me in all things to rely upon Your holy will. In every hour of the day, reveal Your will to me. Bless my dealings with all who surround me. Teach me to treat all that comes to me throughout the day with peace of soul and with firm conviction that Your will governs all. In all my deeds and words, guide my thoughts and feelings. In unforeseen events, let me not forget that all are sent by You. Teach me to act firmly and wisely, without

embittering and embarrassing others. Grant me strength to bear the fatigue of the coming day with all that it shall bring. Direct my will, teach me to pray, and You, Yourself, pray in me. Amen.

You could memorize a few special psalms and recite them (see Appendix II for a handy list of comforting psalms). My Grandma, Hazel Phipps, used to recite Psalms 121 and 23 by heart and pray by name for all her loved ones as she rode her stationary bike every morning. She lived to the ripe age of ninety-four. (I'm not saying that's why she lived so long, but I'm not saying that wasn't the reason, either.)

You could set twenty minutes aside each evening to silently pray the Jesus Prayer: "Lord Jesus Christ, Son of God, have mercy on me, a sinner." Or simply pray "Lord, have mercy." Prayer is the fountain of patience and peace. Whatever you decide to do will be a blessing. I know it is hard to have the discipline to pray, but I believe you can do it. Lord, teach us to pray!

Grief Wisdom for Week Two

FROM SCRIPTURE

Jesus said to her, "I am the resurrection and the life. He who believes in Me, though he may die, he shall live. And whoever lives and believes in Me shall never die. Do you believe this?" (John 11:25–26)

FROM LITURGY

Come, let us bestow the final kiss on the one death has taken, who has now departed from us and proceeds to his resting place, no longer troubled over the things of this world. . . . As we part, let us pray that the Lord grant him eternal rest. (Orthodox Funeral Service)

FROM THE SAINTS

All shall be well,
and all shall be well,
and all manner of thing shall be well. (Julian of Norwich)[120]

FROM CULTURE/LITERATURE

Were it possible for us to see further than our knowledge reaches, and yet a little way beyond the outworks of our divinings, perhaps we would endure our sadnesses with greater confidence than our joys. For they are the moments when something new has entered into us, something unknown; our feelings grow mute in shy perplexity, everything in us withdraws, a stillness comes, and the new, which no one knows, stands in the midst of it and is silent. (Rainer Maria Rilke)[121]

FROM A GRIEVING ORTHODOX CHRISTIAN

Priscilla: My mother was a dancer, and she had great timing! To die during Holy Week, and to have her funeral on Bright Monday? Could that be more perfect? Basically all we sang was "Christ is Risen!" It was so joyful and bright. And now [the hymn] "The Angel Cried" has so much depth to it.

Your Community

Meeting Agenda

OPENING: TRISAGION PRAYERS

GROUP CHECK-IN

How are you coping this week?

GOSPEL READING: MARK 16:9–20

Stand together and choose one participant to read the Gospel aloud.

QUESTIONS FOR DISCUSSION

1. Who is your community? Is it your parish, your friends, your immediate family, your coworkers? What did people say to you after your loved one died? In a time of grief, people often offer helpful and unhelpful words of consolation.

2. **Shift Response versus Support Response**
   Often when people share with us something difficult they're

going through, our instinct is to respond by mentioning some similar situation in our own life. Our intention is to let the other person know they're not alone, but the effect is often to shut down the conversation, making the distressed person feel they're not being heard. This is the "shift response"—shifting the conversation to talk about ourselves.

A better approach is the "support response," in which we invite the distressed person to talk more about whatever is bothering them. Allowing someone to talk through their emotions is often the kindest and most supportive thing we can do.

EXERCISE

Share one example of a helpful or supportive action or comment that your friends or family have offered you in your time of grief. If people have said or done hurtful or unhelpful things, you may want to share them as well.

CLOSING: PRAYER OF THE HOURS

On Your Own

GRIEF ACTIVITY: REACH OUT TO A FRIEND

Between Weeks Three and Four, I would like you to consider texting, calling, or emailing a trusted friend, even if you don't really feel like it. Maybe you could grab coffee or go for a walk. Maybe you could ask him or her for some small, specific help, like picking up groceries or walking your dog. Or you could ask your friend to bring you some ice cream or take you for a drive in the countryside.

Our friends and loved ones truly want to help us when we are grieving, but they may be hesitant to bother us or invade our privacy (which is a bit silly, but it's honestly what they think). They might even say kind things like, "Please let me know what I can do to help." So, this week, you should take them up on that offer and tell them what you need. Be bold! They want to help.

Grief Wisdom for Week Three

FROM SCRIPTURE

Therefore we do not lose heart. Even though our outward man is perishing, yet the inward man is being renewed day by day. For our light affliction, which is but for a moment, is working for us a far more exceeding and eternal weight of glory, while we do not look at the things which are seen, but at the things which are not seen. For the things which are seen are temporary, but the things which are not seen are eternal. (2 Cor. 4:16–18)

FROM LITURGY

Where is the desire of the world? Where is the pomp of the temporal? Where are the gold and the silver? Where is all the gathering and noise of friends? . . . Let us pray to the Immortal King: O Lord, deem the one departed from us worthy of your eternal blessing and give him rest in the everlasting happiness of heaven. (Orthodox Funeral Service)

FROM THE SAINTS

I was wholly at peace, at ease and at rest, so that there was nothing upon earth which could have afflicted me. This lasted only for a time, and then I was changed. I felt there was no ease or comfort for me except faith, hope, and love, and truly I felt very little of this. And then presently God gave me comfort and rest for my soul . . . and then again I felt the pain and then afterwards the delight and the joy, now the one and now the other, again and again, I suppose about twenty times. (Julian of Norwich)[122]

FROM CULTURE/LITERATURE

What I need to hear from you is that you recognize how painful it is. To comfort me, you have to come close. Come sit beside me on my mourning bench. (Nicholas Wolterstorff)[123]

FROM A GRIEVING ORTHODOX CHRISTIAN

Leonard: Someone said—and this was helpful—that this grief would be like a wound, and there are times when it will open up again. It's true, and now that I've had more time to process it, I felt stuff I'd never felt before.

Memory Eternal

Meeting Agenda

OPENING: TRISAGION PRAYERS

GROUP CHECK-IN

How are you coping this week?

GOSPEL READING: LUKE 24:12–35

Stand together and choose one participant to read the Gospel aloud.

QUESTIONS FOR DISCUSSION

1. In Orthodox Christian prayers for our departed loved ones, we say, "May their memory be eternal." Saying "memory eternal" implies that we pray for loved ones, whom we hold in our abiding love. We also believe that "memory eternal" is not only our human memory, but also God's memory of us. What does "memory eternal" mean to you?

2. Do you pray for your loved one? Why or why not?

3. What do you miss most about your loved one, and what can you do to keep that memory alive?

CLOSING: PRAYER OF THE HOURS

On Your Own
GRIEF ACTIVITY: REMEMBRANCE BOX

Between Weeks Four and Five, consider creating a Remembrance Box. This is a special box where you can store cherished items that remind you of your loved one. There are nearly infinite possibilities of what it can hold: a handwritten note, an old photograph, a piece of jewelry, a bowtie, a scrap of fabric, anything. It's a box that you can open and look through any time you need to feel connected to your loved one. You could even ask friends and family to write memories on pieces of paper, and you could store them inside. We need these small rituals. It's beautiful and comforting to have something tangible that reminds you of your loved one.

Grief Wisdom for Week Four
FROM SCRIPTURE

"Let not your heart be troubled; you believe in God, believe also in Me. In My Father's house are many mansions; if it were not so, I would have told you. I go to prepare a place for you. And if I go and prepare a place for you, I will come again and receive you to Myself; that where I am, there you may be also. And where I go you know, and the way you know." Thomas said to

Him, "Lord, we do not know where You are going, and how can we know the way?" Jesus said to him, "I am the way, the truth, and the life. No one comes to the Father except through Me." (John 14:1–6)

FROM LITURGY

O God of spirits and of all flesh, You trampled upon death and abolished the power of the devil, giving life to Your world. Give rest to the soul of Your departed servant in a place of light, in a place of green pasture, in a place of refreshment, from where pain, sorrow, and sighing have fled away. As a good and loving God, forgive every sin he/she has committed in word, deed, or thought, for there is no one who lives and does not sin. You alone are without sin. Your righteousness is an everlasting righteousness, and Your word is truth. (Orthodox Memorial Service)

FROM THE SAINTS

In all paths on which people must journey in this world, they will find no peace unless they draw near to the hope which is in God. (Saint Isaac the Syrian)[124]

FROM CULTURE/LITERATURE

Real grief is not healed by time . . . if time does anything, it deepens our grief. The longer we live, the more fully we become aware of who she was for us, and the more intimately we experience what her love meant for us. Real, deep love is, as you know, very unobtrusive, seemingly easy and obvious, and so present that we take it for granted. Therefore, it is often only in retrospect—or better, in memory—that we fully realize its power and depth. (Henri Nouwen)[125]

FROM A GRIEVING ORTHODOX CHRISTIAN

Quinn: Not too long ago I found out that "memory eternal" is not just that you remember someone, but are remembered by God. In remembering, we remember death, and we remember that God loves us, He always loves us. I love the person I'm singing for, and if I don't particularly know the person, then it's about how God loves us.

Continuing Bonds

Meeting Agenda

OPENING: TRISAGION PRAYERS

GROUP CHECK-IN

How are you coping this week?

GOSPEL READING: LUKE 24:36–53

QUESTIONS FOR DISCUSSION

1. Do you feel that you have an ongoing relationship with your loved one? Psychologists have described this concept as having "continuing bonds." The Orthodox Christian tradition has always encouraged prayerful continuing bonds as we pray for loved ones and believe they pray for us. What kind of ongoing relationship do you hope for?

2. Is there an unresolved need for healing or forgiveness in your relationship with your departed loved one?

3. Picture your loved one in your mind. What would he or she say to you right now to bring you comfort? Do you believe she or he prays for you? What might he or she being praying for?

CLOSING: PRAYER OF THE HOURS

On Your Own

GRIEF ACTIVITY: LETTER TO YOUR LOVED ONE

Between Weeks Five and Six, I offer you the activity of writing a letter to your loved one. This is widely understood to be a therapeutic practice. It's not for anyone else to read. Be honest and brave, and please say what you need to say. (You could even set it aflame—safely—when you are done, as a way to let go of the sentiments you've written.)

If you are angry with your loved one for leaving you, say so. If you are lonely, say this. If you are worried about what's next for you, write that. Express what is going on inside your heart and mind, and don't censor yourself. I believe you will find this helpful and even cathartic. If you would like an additional follow-up activity, consider writing a reply letter to yourself from your loved one. If it sounds odd—it's not. You may find a surprising amount of insight into your grief if you take a step back and let the departed one speak to you. Again, don't censor yourself. You know him or her. Let him or her speak to your heart. This can be a surprisingly beautiful way to hear the voice of your loved one again.

Grief Wisdom for Week Five

FROM SCRIPTURE

Peace I leave with you, My peace I give to you; not as the world gives do I give to you. Let not your heart be troubled, neither let it be afraid. You have heard Me say to you, "I am going away and coming back to you." If you loved Me, you would rejoice because I said, "I am going to the Father," for My Father is greater than I. (John 14:27–28)

FROM LITURGY

Rejoice, through whom joy shall shine forth; rejoice, through whom the curse shall vanish. Rejoice, fallen Adam's restoration; rejoice, redemption of Eve's tears. Rejoice, height that is too difficult for human thought to ascend; rejoice, depth that is too strenuous for angels' eyes to perceive; rejoice, for you are the throne of the King; rejoice, for you hold Him who sustains everything. Rejoice, star that shows forth the Sun; rejoice, womb in which God became incarnate. Rejoice, through whom creation is renewed; rejoice, through whom the Creator becomes an infant. Rejoice, O Bride unwedded! (Akathist Hymn to the Theotokos)

FROM THE SAINTS

The Lord Himself will teach us how to pray. We won't learn prayer on our own, nor will anyone else teach us it. Don't let's say to ourselves, "I have made such-and-such a number of prostrations, so now I have secured divine grace," but rather let us make entreaty for the pure light of divine knowledge to shine within us and open our spiritual eyes so that we may understand His divine words. (St. Porphyrios)[126]

FROM A GRIEVING ORTHODOX CHRISTIAN

Leonard: I have so many incredible examples of my dad reaching out to us since his death. He was a multi-instrumentalist and played with a ton of musicians in the seventies and eighties. To me, his voice wasn't his speaking voice. It was his oboe, his English horn, his clarinet. Any time I hear him on the radio, it's like he is speaking to me. For example, on the day of his death, we had a long drive back home, to prepare for the funeral. And bingo, in the car on the radio, there was his English horn solo on [a world-famous pop singer's] song. It was like he was with us!

Forgiveness, Anger, and Self-Care

Meeting Agenda

OPENING: TRISAGION PRAYERS

GROUP CHECK-IN

How are you coping this week?

GOSPEL READING: JOHN 20:19–31

QUESTIONS FOR DISCUSSION

1. We are made in the image and likeness of God. We are whole people: body, mind, spirit. Have you been prioritizing spiritual, physical, and mental care for yourself?

2. Do you ask others for help? Are there a few trusted loved ones you can talk to? We can all agree it is crucial to take care of yourself during a time of grief. Can you be honest about your struggles with a trusted loved one?

3. How is your prayer life? Are you attending church and taking part in the sacramental life of faith? Why or why not?

CLOSING: PRAYER OF THE HOURS

On Your Own

GRIEF ACTIVITY: WRITING A SELF-CARE PLAN

Between Weeks Six and Seven, I request that you assess your overall well-being and self-care. The term "self-care" gets thrown around a lot these days, but it is important. Take a hard look at your daily life and touch base with your physician for a checkup. Are you getting enough sleep? Eating appropriately? Drinking enough water? Spending too much money? Drinking more alcohol or using drugs?

Review the areas that need work and take specific steps to work on this. Your health matters. What are three concrete ways you can improve your self-care? Examples: going to bed earlier, asking your friend for a ride to church, making sure you have healthy food in your home, taking a daily walk, sharing your feelings with a therapist, going to your physician to discuss a health concern, setting aside quiet time, setting limits with others, learning to say no, and prioritizing joyful activities like dancing or going to concerts.

Grief Wisdom for Week Six

FROM SCRIPTURE

For if we live, we live to the Lord; and if we die, we die to the Lord. Therefore, whether we live or die, we are the Lord's. For to this end Christ died and rose and lives again, that He might be Lord of both the dead and the living. (Romans 14:8–9)

FROM LITURGY

When the trumpet will sound again the dead will rise as in a quake to greet You, O Christ God. At that time, grant, O Lord, that the one You have taken from us, the soul of Your servant, be in fellowship with the saints. (Orthodox Funeral Service)

FROM THE SAINTS

See whom He calls! Those who have spent their strength in breaking the law, those who are burdened with their sins, those who can no longer lift up their heads, those who are filled with shame, those who can no longer speak out. And why does He call them? . . . To relieve them from their pain, to take away their heavy burden. (St. John Chrysostom)[127]

FROM CULTURE/LITERATURE

A friend came in one day to visit a retired bishop who was in a home for terminal cancer patients. "How are you doing?" he asked. The bishop replied, "I'm just sitting here letting God love me." Why not do the same as you grieve? Just sit there in God's presence and let God love you as you grieve. Is He not closer to you than the air you breathe? And who loves you more than God? And do you not belong to Him by right of creation as well as by right of redemption? Let God love you. Let God grieve with you. (Anthony Coniaris)[128]

FROM A GRIEVING ORTHODOX CHRISTIAN

Chris: I sit with Our Lady of Sorrows, the Theotokos icon. I sit with the icon of Christ as the Bridegroom. I hear the lamentations, for Dormition and Pascha. That is so healing. I still had the grief to go through, but you don't have the sense of being alone.

How Grief Can Challenge Our Faith

Meeting Agenda

OPENING: TRISAGION PRAYERS

GROUP CHECK-IN

How are you coping this week?

GOSPEL READING: JOHN 21:1–14

QUESTIONS FOR DISCUSSION

1. Grief can be the most painful process you have experienced in your life. It grants you a certain kind of empathy and spiritual wisdom—maybe a wisdom you didn't want. How has your faith changed in the wake of your grief?

2. Have you ever felt angry at God? Have you ever had a time where you couldn't pray or talk to God?

3. When or where do you feel closest to God? What do you do

when you can't feel God's presence? How do you reconnect with God?

CLOSING: PRAYER OF THE HOURS

On Your Own

GRIEF ACTIVITY: AN ACT OF KINDNESS

One of the easiest ways to reconnect with God is to do an act of kindness for others. Between Weeks Seven and Eight, I challenge you to do something special for someone else—a loved one or a stranger, anonymously or not. The possibilities are many. You could pay for someone's coffee in the drive-through. You could play the piano at a senior center, or surprise your spouse with dinner and a movie, or rake your neighbor's leaves. You could buy (or knit) a bunch of warm hats and socks and give them to homeless people on the street. You could make a monetary donation to a worthy cause. You could buy lunch for people at your office (and you could even do it anonymously! How fun!). The goal is to do one small thing that brings joy to others. You may find that it puts a smile on your face as well and gives you a moment of grace and peace. Thank you in advance for sharing your love with others!

Grief Wisdom for Week Seven

FROM SCRIPTURE

Not that I speak in regard to need, for I have learned in whatever state I am, to be content: I know how to be abased, and I know how to abound. Everywhere and in all things I have learned both to be full and to be hungry, both to abound and to suffer need. I can do all things through Christ who strengthens me. (Phil. 4:11–13)

FROM LITURGY

Lord God Almighty, You alone are holy. You accept the sacrifice of praise from those who call upon You with their whole heart, even so, accept from us sinners our supplication, and bring it to Your holy Altar of sacrifice. Enable us to offer You gifts and spiritual sacrifices for our own sins and the failings of Your people. Deem us worthy to find grace in Your sight, that our sacrifice may be well pleasing to You, and that the good Spirit of Your grace may rest upon us and upon these gifts presented and upon all Your people. Through the mercies of Your only-begotten Son, with whom You are blessed, together with Your all-holy, good, and life-creating Spirit, now and forever and to the ages of ages. Amen. (The Divine Liturgy of St. John Chrysostom)

FROM THE SAINTS

Go on in all simplicity; do not be anxious to win a quiet mind, and it will be all the quieter. Do not examine so closely into the progress of your soul. Do not crave so much to be perfect, but let your spiritual life be formed by your duties, and by the actions which are called forth by circumstances. Do not take overmuch thought for tomorrow. God, who has led you safely on so far, will lead you on to the end. (Francis de Sales)[129]

FROM A GRIEVING ORTHODOX CHRISTIAN

Irene: It deepened my faith. I remember the finite nature of my own life, and I think about meeting God at my death. I'm approaching the "no green bananas" stage. I want to be prepared. And the loss deepened my sense of the limitations of being human, and the love of God, the overseeing of God. It helped me see the previous limits of my faith, and that actually we are swimming in an ocean of God! Everything is from God. Everything!

Bright Sadness

Meeting Agenda

OPENING: TRISAGION PRAYERS

GROUP CHECK-IN

How are you coping this week?

GOSPEL READING: JOHN 21:15–25

QUESTIONS FOR DISCUSSION

1. Orthodox Christians often use the terms "bright sadness" or "joyful sorrow" to capture our unified sense of Christ's crucifixion and resurrection, and His death and life. What does bright sadness mean to you?

2. How has your grief changed you as a person? What advice would you give to others who are new to their grief?

3. Please share with the group three things you are thankful for.

CLOSING: PRAYER OF THE HOURS

On Your Own

GRIEF ACTIVITY: SAY THEIR NAMES

Our deceased loved ones have names—beautiful names, names that have meaning and heritage and strength. Let us say their names whenever we can. Talk about them; tell all the ridiculous stories, say what you miss about them, and remember them in your words and your deeds. You know how important it is to hear your loved one's name.

Now, take this pearl of wisdom and bring it to your greater community. When you see a widow at church, tell her something you liked about her late husband. When you see your cousin who is facing her own grief, tell her, "I miss your mom." When your friend has a new baby, acknowledge that it must be hard not to have her dad around to meet the baby. Say what's in your heart and help others do the same. When we say the names of our departed, it is a brave and loving act. You know that you will never forget your loved one. Help others know that their loved ones are not forgotten either.

Grief Wisdom for Week Eight

FROM SCRIPTURE

But I do not want you to be ignorant, brethren, concerning those who have fallen asleep, lest you sorrow as others who have no hope. For if we believe that Jesus died and rose again, even so God will bring with Him those who sleep in Jesus. For this we say to you by the word of the Lord, that we who are alive and remain until the coming of the Lord will by no means precede those who are asleep. For the Lord Himself will descend from heaven with a shout, with the voice of an archangel, and with the trumpet of God. And the dead in Christ will rise first. Then we who are alive and remain shall be caught up together with them in the clouds to meet the Lord in the air. And thus we shall always be with the Lord. Therefore comfort one another with these words. (1 Thess. 4:13–18)

FROM LITURGY

Having beheld the resurrection of Christ, let us worship the holy Lord Jesus, the only sinless One. We venerate Your Cross, O Christ, and we praise and glorify Your holy resurrection; for You are our God and we know no other than You. We call on Your name. O Come all ye faithful, let us venerate Christ's holy resurrection! For behold, through the cross joy has come into all the world. Let us ever bless the Lord, praising His resurrection. For by enduring the cross for us, He has destroyed death by death. (Paschal Matins)

FROM METROPOLITAN ANTHONY

One should never say, "We loved one another." We should always say, "We love one another." Love cannot be corrupted by death.[130]

FROM A GRIEVING ORTHODOX CHRISTIAN

Sasha: I believe, we believe, that no matter how beautiful our liturgy is, our music is, it doesn't compare to where I hope [he] is. He hasn't missed anything! If anything, we are the ones missing out!

Anna: My friend wore all white to her husband's funeral, and when everyone kept saying, "I'm sorry, I'm sorry," she replied over and over with "Christ is Risen!" That's all you can say, that's all you need to say. So that's what I did when [my husband] died. I wore a white dress, and I said "Christ is risen!"

TRULY, THAT IS ALL we collectively need to say. Our faith, given by God, reaches into the depths of grief, and our liturgical practices help us experience the many facets of loss. Our faith allows for a full expression of loss, including joy, sorrow, silence, connection, and peace. Both personally and communally, the faith teaches us how to nourish a grieving heart and how to grow as Christians in the midst of joyful sorrow. May God bless you, both now and ever, and unto ages of ages. Amen.

Conclusion

To live as Christians requires an ongoing discernment of the needs of the people in our parishes and our broader communities. In this book, I have attempted to synthesize our rich and meaningful tradition with new and dynamic ways to care for the grieving. I am guided by the gift of liturgy that we inherit as Orthodox faithful, our belief in God's love for us, and a communal trust that God moves and speaks to us in new ways.

As Orthodox Christians, we live in constant discernment of the Holy Spirit in the Church, and we are guided by living tradition. It is precisely this conversation with the past that has guided my firm belief that we all grieve, we all suffer, and we all can find healing and wholeness in the community of faith. In the time of grief, when painful truths are often left unspoken, we must pray the words we have been given by a long line of saints, our fellow Christians. In these words, we find healing and wholeness. We do not grieve alone. We find solace sitting with other people, sharing in our grief and our joy, ever focused on the One "in whose light we shall see light," as we hear in the Divine Liturgy.

The life of faith requires a certain openness to allowing God to work within us. When we are at our most vulnerable, we must remain open to that "still, small voice" of God that speaks in what feels like a vast silence. We allow ourselves to be surprised by God's voice and the voices of others who accompany us in grief.

C. S. Lewis has shared his experiences of healing amidst the grief of losing his wife. He writes, "Something quite unexpected has happened . . . my heart was lighter than it had been for many weeks . . . and suddenly, I remembered her best."[131] His memory of his wife became palpable, and he experienced "something (almost) better than memory; an instantaneous, unanswerable impression. To say it was like a meeting would be going too far. Yet there was that in it which tempts one to use those words."[132] Memory is powerful, and memory is woven profoundly into our lives when we grieve.

Our own memories sustain us and offer us peace, consolation, and connection. But most importantly, we are held in God's memory. Whether we live or we die, we are held in His memory, His body. God's memory is eternal, in a manner that is beyond any understanding and yet deeply known in our heart of hearts. God is with us.

We live in an Orthodox Christian balance of firm beliefs and just as firm acknowledgment that our understanding of life, death, and the world is limited. We do our best to discern God's love in our lives. When we suffer, we turn our hearts to God and hold space for each other, with patience and love. We do this humbly, with wisdom inherited from our tradition, guided by those who have come before us. We ask difficult questions, and we reach out to one another in prayer and fellowship and thanksgiving. We light candles for our loved ones who have died, and we pray for them by name in liturgy, knowing their names are known and remembered by the Lord. We leave space for mystery.

If we wonder whether our prayers matter, we hear the words of Fr. Schmemann reminding us that "whether our prayers for our departed loved ones bring any benefit to them is a question we must leave to the mercy of God. But of one thing we are certain: such prayers do benefit those who pray for the departed."[133] Further, he reminds us, "They make us more cautious and diligent in getting ready for that ultimate journey which will unite us with our departed loved ones and usher us into the presence of God."[134] Our journey of grief teaches us about the nature of our lives within God's kingdom, both here on earth and in the place of repose and rest with Christ. May God grant that we may continue to care for each other in new ways that attend to the suffering and grief of our neighbors. We pray together as one voice, "With the saints give rest, O Christ, to the souls of Thy servants, where there is no pain, no sorrow, no sighing, but life everlasting." May the memory of all our loved ones be eternal. Christ is Risen!

Group Facilitator's Guide

TO BEGIN, WE would like to thank you for considering leading a Memory Eternal Bereavement Group. What a gift you are giving to your community! We are hopeful it will be spiritually fruitful and life-giving for you as well.

Grief can be profoundly lonely. Processing grief requires the compassion and loving support of other human beings. It calls for gentle listening, openheartedness, patience, and kindness. It requires deep emotional work, vulnerability, and a willingness to share with others. Companioning others in the process of grief could be considered one of the most fundamental, life-giving calls that God offers to us.

Your ministry as a bereavement group facilitator is a loving witness to your faith in Christ. As we see in Holy Scripture, "Pure and undefiled religion before God and the Father is this: to visit orphans and widows in their trouble" (James 1:27). Thank you for practicing religion at its best: loving and caring for God's orphans, widows, widowers, and all those who are bereaved.

Who Can Facilitate the Group?

Any interested Orthodox Christian, whether lay or ordained, male or female, can lead a Memory Eternal group. You don't need a degree in counseling, and you don't need to have a personal history of bereavement. The qualifications for a facilitator are that you:

1. are a practicing Orthodox Christian in good standing with your parish;
2. are committed to following the group guidelines;
3. are a good listener, not dominating conversation;
4. have the blessing of your priest; and
5. have a heart that is open to the love of God and neighbor.

Christ calls all of us to some form of loving ministry: "He Himself gave some to be apostles, some prophets, some evangelists, and some pastors and teachers, for the equipping of the saints for the work of ministry, for the edifying of the body of Christ, till we all come to the unity of the faith and of the knowledge of the Son of God, to a perfect man, to the measure of the stature of the fullness of Christ" (Eph. 4:11–13). Those who are called to listen and support others may discern an important ministry as a facilitator of a bereavement group.

Every bereavement group needs a designated facilitator, or two if possible. The groups should not run themselves. As the facilitator, you will guide the flow of the group, move the conversation through the reflection questions, open and close the meeting at the arranged times, address special concerns raised within the group, and try to recognize when a group member needs a referral to individual counseling.

Remember, you are there to hold the space for reflection and to gently encourage the group's discussion. You are not there to provide answers or fix someone's grief—though it's so very tempting to try to fix difficult or uncomfortable emotions. Instead, let the questions and readings guide the group discussion. Holding a compassionate and accepting place for people to share, connect, and ask questions in the supportive context of our faith in Christ can be profoundly meaningful. Your only agenda should be to guide the group in discussion and let the fellowship and connection in God be the source of healing.

A word to the wise: remember that the bereavement group experience might not be everyone's cup of tea. Some participants might decide that the group is not helpful for them. They will be subjected to the grief stories of others, and if this sadness is too much to bear, the group will not be a healing experience. Additionally, each group member has less time to speak than with individual therapy. As the facilitator, you can identify this for the group and keep an eye on the dynamics. Try not to take it personally if the group doesn't work out for someone. Remember that you can always privately recommend that your participant follow up directly with his or her priest and/or a licensed therapist.

A Quick Guide to Starting Up the Group

1. Register all participants in advance. The group may meet in person or online.

2. One facilitator is required, but you may have two facilitators if available.

3. Limit the group to eight participants, plus the facilitator(s).

4. The meeting may be up to one and a half hours long. Please start and end on time.

5. The individual group members should purchase this book for themselves in advance. Please do not photocopy the bereavement guide.

6. If you are meeting in person, the meeting room should have comfortable seating, with chairs arranged in a circle, boxes of tissues, an icon for prayer, and water and/or coffee. Put signs up to direct the group members to the meeting room, and provide name tags for all group members.

7. Stick to the bereavement group guide.

8. Ask your priest to pray for you and your group during liturgy.

How Is a Support Group Unique?

There are various types of bereavement-related groups, including therapeutic, self-help, and support groups, and they have key differences both in leadership and content. A therapeutic group is for people who have identified that they have specific personal problems that affect their grieving. This type of group is overseen by a credentialed professional, such as a social worker or mental health counselor. A self-help group is self-led by people experiencing grief. The focus of such a group might be on practical issues of bereavement, such as daily coping, making schedules, and tips for living with grief. Such groups do not have a primary focus on processing the emotional or spiritual complexities of grief.

Memory Eternal bereavement groups are support groups,

not therapeutic or self-help. Our group focuses on the practical, emotional, spiritual, and relational aspects of grief. To be clear: groups do not take the place of private therapy. If a member of your group appears to be fully overwhelmed by grief (for example, he or she cannot stop crying, cannot sleep, or is not able to self-regulate) and his or her grief appears to be significantly affecting his or her overall health, a therapeutic group or private counseling may be needed.[135] An immediate referral to a mental health professional and/or physician is strongly recommended if a participant arrives to the group under the influence of drugs or alcohol, communicates thoughts of suicide or self-harm, acts out in sudden or dramatic ways within the group, or suggests that he or she is unable to care for him- or herself properly. These situations are beyond the scope of your practice as a group facilitator and require referral.

There are at least two types of bereavement groups: open and closed. Open groups run on an ongoing basis, such as the first Sunday of the month or every Wednesday. They are drop-in and do not generally have a set curriculum. The Memory Eternal group is closed, meaning it has a set duration and a specific group of people who sign up in advance. This closed group offers a mix of educational, spiritual, and emotional support. It runs for eight weeks, at a time and day which you and your parish determine to be suitable, whether a weeknight, a Sunday afternoon, or a lunch time. The meetings should be one and a half hours long. Please adhere to the advertised beginning and ending times; for those who are grieving, structure and timeliness can provide a bit of much-needed stability and predictability.

The module for each week consists of:

1. Opening prayers
2. Group check-in
3. Gospel reading
4. Discussion questions and exercises
5. Closing prayers

Please use the guide to focus the discussion on the topics for the week.

In addition to the meeting agenda, participants can use the following on their own between meetings:

6. Grief activity
7. Grief words of wisdom, including quotes from Scripture, liturgy, the saints, modern culture and literature, and grieving Orthodox Christians.

Ideally, the curriculum may be used at any parish, at any time of year. It may be integrated into the life of the community, and it allows for demographic variations and cultural differences. It is Orthodox Christian at its core; it is specific enough to be meaningful but general enough to appeal to different communities and demographics.

When I researched and designed this curriculum, I reflected on whether participation should be limited to Orthodox Christians. As I interviewed grieving Orthodox Christians and consulted with my peers and clergy colleagues, the consensus became clear: the group should be open to any interested party, beyond the confines of the parish, with registration. First, this is simply practical; publicizing the group beyond the parish means it is more likely to attain enough participants. The group is clear about its Orthodox basis for meaning-making; this shared worldview will keep the group grounded and centered in Christ while allowing for diverse experiences.

This is also an opportunity for compassionate outreach and evangelism to the community. What a profound way to support and care for anyone who is grieving! In this secular age of increasing alienation from community, the powerful message of a group like this is that all are welcome, all are invited to a life-giving relationship with Christ and with our neighbors, and that healing is found in engaging a life of faith. I encourage any interested parishes to offer this opportunity for learning and connection to all those who grieve in the community.

Participants will hear others' opinions and points of view that are similar to and different from their own. They will be able to assess their situations in light of wisdom from peers who share their worldview. They may be able to reassure themselves that they are not going crazy. They set a structured time to get out of the house and connect with others (or do so virtually). They may be able to discuss concerns or topics in the group that they would not raise with family or friends. It is a safe place wherein the group members commit to shared guidelines, which are described in Week One. The continuity of social, emotional, and sacramental connection builds up the community of the parish and the greater local Orthodox community in a special way.

Notably, the social and emotional connections made in the group come to fruition when participants are worshiping together, praying together, and receiving Holy Communion together. We view worship in the eucharistic gathering as the center of our faith. Those we worship alongside—whether strangers or neighbors—are our brothers and sisters in the family of the Church. So often, the social connections to parish members are limited to a brief conversation at coffee hour. How much more profound it could be to understand the grief and the needs of those standing around you—to pass the peace not merely as strangers, but truly as neighbors.

Understanding Group Dynamics

There is power and wisdom within a group process. Irving Yalom, the psychologist, theorized that a group provides a connection with others; an opportunity to help others; hope from seeing others "get better"; a feeling of belonging and universal acceptance; and universality of feelings.[136] He also highlighted the importance of interpersonal relationships; though we live in relationship with others, we all fear loneliness. This fear can be lessened within a supportive group.

A group can be a vehicle for people to identify and deal with their own emotional blocks and limitations. The successful group participant not only develops an improved capacity to relate to others but also more inner comfort and a far better ability to realize his or her own potential. As the group facilitator, you help with "culture building," or setting the tone for the group. You should keep an eye out for interpersonal dynamics in order to hold space for each participant and to keep the conversation flowing.

You may try open-ended responses such as "Tell me more" or "What was that like for you?" To keep the pace of the group moving along, you could say, "I'm mindful of the time, and I want to make sure we get to the discussion questions. Would that be okay with everyone?" Be as clear and straightforward as possible.

Sometimes group participants fall into roles that can affect the overall dynamic. These roles might include the monopolist who talks too much, the silent member who backs away from dialogue, the boring person who resorts to clichés and apologies, and the help-rejecting complainer who takes pride in the insolubility of her problems. If group members fall into these roles, you can respond with curiosity, compassion, and intentional invitation into dialogue.

For example, to a monopolist, you might say, "John, I really appreciate what you've been sharing. I also want to make sure we have time to hear other people's experiences." To a silent member, you might say, "Adrian, I notice you've been quiet, and that is absolutely fine with us. However, please know that we want to hear your thoughts and ideas, whenever you're ready." To the person who resorts to clichés, you might say, "Rafael, it sounds like you've shared a lot of the common phrases we hear about grief. Do they actually resonate with you?" And to the help-rejecting complainer, you might say, "Camilla, I hear how hard this has been for you, and it seems you feel that nothing has helped or changed your outlook. I wonder if some of the techniques in the guide might address your grief in a new way."

You may also find you have an armchair theologian or two in your group. This can be particularly tricky, because though they are often well-intended, religious platitudes might be theologically inaccurate ("God needed another angel in heaven"), emotionally hurtful ("Everything happens for a reason"), or just plain unkind ("God doesn't give you anything you can't handle"). No individual within the group should be offering theological consultation or pastoral advice to another member. If you hear these kinds of comments, gently steer the group back to the conversation guide and make a strong recommendation that all complex theological questions be directed to clergy.

What Should I Say? Naming the Here and Now

If you feel like the group is stuck or the conversation is not flowing well, consider the facilitation concept of *activating the here and now*. This may sound complicated, but it is not rocket science; it is simply noticing and naming emotions and responses in the moment. If someone is crying, you might say, "I can tell this is so heartbreaking for you." If someone is struggling to find words to describe their experience, you might say, "I imagine this is so hard for you. Take all the time you need." If someone's body language appears frustrated or upset, you might say, "I wonder if this makes you angry." It is compassionate to notice and acknowledge difficult emotions as they are occurring. By doing so, you can normalize healthy emotional expressions within the group.

One technique for this here-and-now approach is called *emotional bridging*. Bridging involves encouraging people to expose their inner reflections with one another. You may use bridging to evoke connections between group participants. In such connections, group members offer insight and wisdom to fellow members and develop courage and strength while recognizing that they are not alone.

There are several ways to employ bridging. For example, you can use an open-ended question, which is one that can be answered in many ways. The most common form is asking one group member what he or she imagines another member is feeling. This method establishes a bridge by encouraging one person to attempt to understand another. For example, you might ask Skye, "What do you think Rachel is feeling when she hunches over like that?" and Skye might say, "She feels like there's no point to all this talking!" Rachel may be pleasantly surprised by Skye's insight, and Skye may recognize this previously unnamed feeling within herself.

Another bridging method is asking a question so a member can find someone else's "feeling-double." For example, imagine a group wherein one member, Carine, has regularly expressed painful feelings about losing her husband at a young age. Rather than calling on her directly, we may call upon her "feeling-double," Simona, who has not been as verbally open about her loss. We might say, "Simona, what do you make of all the things Carine says about her husband?" Simona might surprise the group (and herself) by saying, "I get it. My husband was only 64 when he died. We finally had some time to enjoy each other after retirement, but our life was whisked away," and then continue to share. After this, Simona may verbalize a deepened understanding of her own loss: it wasn't only about her husband being young, it was also that the life she knew was cut short. By asking the more expressive member (Carine) what she made of the other's (Simona's) experience, we open up the truth for both. Carine and Simona are given a chance to see themselves in another person.

Toward a Vision of Orthodox Fellowship

Notably, an Orthodox bereavement group is best seen as a fellowship, with its foundation resting in God. But how does a group become a fellowship? And how might the connections found in a bereavement group connect to the greater, ongoing fellowship of the eucharistic gathering? These questions move us toward a vision of Orthodox bereavement wherein the group is not merely individuals chatting in a circle but a true experience of spiritual fellowship, honesty, and healing.

Our understanding of fellowship—of individual persons in communion—flows directly from our understanding of the Holy Trinity: Father, Son, and Holy Spirit. We see this in the First Epistle of John: "That which we have seen and heard we declare to you, that you also may have fellowship with us; and truly our fellowship is with the Father and with His Son Jesus Christ" (1 John 1:3). We experience fellowship, an embodied experience of communion with others, through the divine. Recall that Christ promised He would not leave us alone after His death and Ascension:

> If you love Me, keep My commandments. And I will pray the Father, and He will give you another Helper, that He may abide with you forever—the Spirit of truth, whom the world cannot receive, because it neither sees Him nor knows Him; but you know Him, for He dwells with you and will be in you. I will not leave you orphans; I will come to you. A little while longer and the world will see Me no more, but you will see Me. Because I live, you will live also. At that day you will know that I am in My Father, and you in Me, and I in you. (John 14:15–20)

True fellowship is made possible through the Holy Spirit, who descended on the apostles at Pentecost: "And they continued steadfastly in the apostles' doctrine and fellowship, in the breaking of bread, and in prayers" (Acts 2:42). For the Orthodox Christian, the ultimate example of *koinonia* is within Holy Communion, which brings us into complete union with Christ and with our brothers and sisters. Just as with the disciples on the road to Emmaus, we know Christ and we know each other in the breaking of the bread.

Hence, in order to bring a group to the level of fellowship, it must be framed within the life of the Church and its prayers. This is why the group begins and ends in prayer. Further, it means we agree to a certain type of *agape*, or Christian charity, in our interactions with one another. This might include a special attention to the fruit of the Spirit: love, joy, peace, patience, kindness, goodness, gentleness, and self-control. It means sharing and speaking with honesty and paying attention to one's emotions and words as they affect others. The connection and closeness forged in an intentional group can be healing. And for us as Orthodox Christians, it is infinitely more healing to forge an intentional group that confesses a bond of love united in Christ.

There are times when you will be confronted with difficult group dynamics. If the group enters unmanageable territory, you should make a referral to professional counseling, the member's physician, and/or the parish priest, if appropriate. We cannot fix or cure every situation. This stance of humility and discernment is key to a bereavement group. You will likely have sessions that feel awkward or challenging. Take heart and simply try to do your best, prayerfully and humbly.

Remember that true healing comes not from you, the group facilitator, or from an individual's psychological insights, but from God, the source of life. Healing arises as the group members process their losses together through the lens of faith, in the context of the life of the Church. There will be more questions than answers, more tears than laughter, and more moments of silence than of certainty. But God's love is infinitely available to us. Just the deceptively simple act of being together, praying together, and holding space for grief is profoundly meaningful. God is with us! Remember that God is the One who heals, forgives, offers mercy, and provides the peace that surpasses understanding. Thank you for giving your community this gift of fellowship and healing, and may God bless your ministry.

APPENDIX II

Verses of Comfort

Psalms of Lamentation and Comfort

PSALM 4:6–8

Lord, lift up the light of Your countenance upon us.
You have put gladness in my heart,
More than in the season that their grain and wine increased.
I will both lie down in peace, and sleep;
For You alone, O Lord, make me dwell in safety.

PSALM 22:19

But You, O Lord, do not be far from Me;
O My Strength, hasten to help Me!

PSALM 27:1, 14

The Lord is my light and my salvation;
Whom shall I fear?
The Lord is the strength of my life;
Of whom shall I be afraid?

. . .

Wait on the Lord;
Be of good courage,
And He shall strengthen your heart.

PSALM 34:18
The Lord *is* near to those who have a broken heart,
And saves such as have a contrite spirit.

PSALM 42:5
Why are you cast down, O my soul?
And *why* are you disquieted within me?
Hope in God, for I shall yet praise Him
For the help of His countenance.

PSALM 51:10–11
Create in me a clean heart, O God,
And renew a steadfast spirit within me.
Do not cast me away from Your presence,
And do not take Your Holy Spirit from me.

PSALM 56:3–4
Whenever I am afraid,
I will trust in You.
In God (I will praise His word),
In God I have put my trust;
I will not fear.

PSALM 77:1

I cried out to God with my voice . . .
And He gave ear to me.

PSALM 121:1–2

I will lift up my eyes to the hills—
From whence comes my help?
My help *comes* from the Lord,
Who made heaven and earth.

PSALM 139:7–10

Where can I go from Your Spirit?
Or where can I flee from Your presence?
If I ascend into heaven, You *are* there;
If I make my bed in hell, behold, You *are* there.
If I take the wings of the morning,
And dwell in the uttermost parts of the sea,
Even there Your hand shall lead me,
And Your right hand shall hold me.

New Testament Quotes of Comfort

MATTHEW 5:4

"Blessed *are* those who mourn,
For they shall be comforted."

LUKE 2:10

Then the angel said to them, "Do not be afraid, for behold, I
bring you good tidings of great joy which will be to all people."

JOHN 14:27

"Peace I leave with you, My peace I give to you; not as the world gives do I give to you. Let not your heart be troubled, neither let it be afraid."

JOHN 16:20

"Most assuredly, I say to you that you will weep and lament, but the world will rejoice; and you will be sorrowful, but your sorrow will be turned into joy."

ROMANS 8:18

For I consider that the sufferings of this present time are not worthy to be compared with the glory which shall be revealed in us.

ROMANS 15:13

Now may the God of hope fill you with all joy and peace in believing, that you may abound in hope by the power of the Holy Spirit.

I CORINTHIANS 15:20–22

But now Christ is risen from the dead, and has become the first fruits of those who have fallen asleep. For since by man came death, by Man also came the resurrection of the dead. For as in Adam all die, even so in Christ all shall be made alive.

2 CORINTHIANS 1:3−4

Blessed be the God and Father of our Lord Jesus Christ, the Father of mercies and God of all comfort, who comforts us in all our tribulation, that we may be able to comfort those who are in any trouble, with the comfort with which we ourselves are comforted by God.

EPHESIANS 4:1−3

I, therefore, the prisoner of the Lord, beseech you to walk worthy of the calling with which you were called, with all lowliness and gentleness, with longsuffering, bearing with one another in love, endeavoring to keep the unity of the Spirit in the bond of peace.

PHILIPPIANS 4:6−8

Be anxious for nothing, but in everything by prayer and supplication, with thanksgiving, let your requests be made known to God; and the peace of God, which surpasses all understanding, will guard your hearts and minds through Christ Jesus. Finally, brethren, whatever things are true, whatever things are noble, whatever things are just, whatever things are pure, whatever things are lovely, whatever things are of good report, if there is any virtue and if there is anything praiseworthy—meditate on these things.

I THESSALONIANS 4:13−14

But I do not want you to be ignorant, brethren, concerning those who have fallen asleep, lest you sorrow as others who have no hope. For if we believe that Jesus died and rose again, even so God will bring with Him those who sleep in Jesus.

2 TIMOTHY 4:7–8

I have fought the good fight, I have finished the race, I have kept the faith. Finally, there is laid up for me the crown of righteousness, which the Lord, the righteous Judge, will give to me on that Day, and not to me only but also to all who have loved His appearing.

HEBREWS 4:15–16

For we do not have a High Priest who cannot sympathize with our weaknesses, but was in all points tempted as we are, yet without sin. Let us therefore come boldly to the throne of grace, that we may obtain mercy and find grace to help in time of need.

1 PETER 1:6–8

In this you greatly rejoice, though now for a little while, if need be, you have been grieved by various trials, that the genuineness of your faith, being much more precious than gold that perishes, though it is tested by fire, may be found to praise, honor, and glory at the revelation of Jesus Christ, whom having not seen you love. Though now you do not see Him, yet believing, you rejoice with joy inexpressible and full of glory, receiving the end of your faith—the salvation of your souls.

REVELATION 21:4

And God will wipe away every tear from their eyes; there shall be no more death, nor sorrow, nor crying. There shall be no more pain, for the former things have passed away.

How to Talk to a Grieving Person

FIRST AND FOREMOST, listen to the grieving person. Listen without judgment, interruption, or advice. Do not compare losses or make someone else's grief about you. Don't ask a widower if he will remarry or a newly bereaved parent if he or she will have another child. Do not literally throw yourself into the arms of a grieving person or hug them too tightly (it's exhausting for them!). Do not force yourself to have an upbeat tone or cheer them up. When in doubt, a gentle touch on the shoulder and compassionate silence are most helpful.

If you live far away, send a handwritten letter or a gift card for local food delivery.

Remember, many grieving people receive a great deal of support immediately after the loss. There is a flurry of activity, outreach, and care. But for many, the hardest time is when the calls and visits have stopped, a month or two after the loss. This can be an important time to reach out to a grieving person, because this may be a particularly lonely time. If you send a message every couple of weeks just to say, "I'm thinking of you and sending you love!" it can be immensely comforting.

Please do not say:

» She is in a better place.

(*How can you say that? A pretty good place for her was here, with me!*)

» That's so horrible. I would never be able to deal with it. You're so strong.

(*I know it's horrible. I didn't have a choice. I am doing the best I can. I don't feel strong.*)

» At least you . . . (were able to have a baby/had a husband/ have other kids).

(*Any statement beginning with "at least" is not particularly empathetic.*)

» Heaven gained an angel.

(*That is not what Orthodox Christians believe about what happens after death.*)

» Everything will be okay.

(*It's easy for you to say that, and it may be true. But right now, everything is not okay.*)

» Time will heal all wounds.

(*While it is true that time can lessen the acute pain of loss, many people feel the pain of grief for a very long time. Grief does not have a timeline. And right now, I'm in pain.*)

» You will get over it.

(*I don't want to forget my loved one. I don't want to let go yet. My grief is not something to "get over." It is something that I'm learning to live with, one day at a time.*)

» It's time to get on with your life.

(*It is up to me to decide what it means to get on with my life. I am my own timekeeper.*)

» Let me know if I can do anything.
   (*Rather than putting the burden on the griever to ask for help, it is better to directly offer specific ways to help: "What can I get you from the store?" "I'm dropping off takeout food—do you have any food restrictions or preferences?" "Tell me what time you can drop your children off for a play date this weekend. We'd love to see them." "I'm going to shovel the snow in your driveway today." "I brought you a coffee." "Do you have plans for Christmas Day? Please join us."*)

Please do say:
» *I care about you.*
» *I don't know what you're going through, but I'm here to listen.*
» *My heart is breaking for you.*
» *We love you and we love [your loved one].*
» *Let's go for a walk on Saturday. Are you free at 6 PM?*
» *Do you want to join us for Thanksgiving?*
» *Did I ever tell you the funny story about [your loved one]?*
» *I think [your loved one] was such a great person (or a kind soul, a good teacher, a beautiful singer, a loving parent, a devoted grandmother, and so forth).*
» *I was thinking about [your loved one] the other day and . . .*
» *Your son looks so much like your husband (or your grand-daughter has the same laugh as your wife, and so forth).*
» *Would you like a quiet space, or food, or a listening ear, or a shoulder to cry on, or someone to watch the kids?*
» *Tell me what you miss about [your loved one].*
» *I am praying for you.*
» *May your loved one's memory be eternal.*

Suggested Reading

Bowlby, John. *Attachment*. Basic Books, 2008.

Bregman, Lucy. *Beyond Silence and Denial: Death and dying reconsidered*. Westminster John Knox Press, 1999.

Cacciatore, Joanne. *Bearing the Unbearable: Love, Loss, and the Heartbreaking Path of Grief*. Somerville, MA: Wisdom Publications, 2017.

Devine, Megan. *It's OK That You're Not OK: Meeting Grief and Loss in a Culture That Doesn't Understand*. Sounds True, 2018.

Doka, Kenneth J., ed. *Disenfranchised Grief: Recognizing hidden sorrow*. Lexington, MA: Lexington Books, 1989.

Doka, K. J. and A. S. Tucci, eds., 2011. *Beyond Kübler-Ross: New perspectives on death, dying and grief*. Washington, DC: Hospice Foundation of America, and Corr, C.A., 2015.

Hickman, Martha Whitmore. *Healing after Loss: Daily meditations for working through grief*. Tantor Media, Incorporated, 2011.

James, John W., and Russell Friedman. *The Grief Recovery Handbook, 20th Anniversary Expanded Edition: The Action Program for Moving Beyond Death, Divorce, and Other Losses including Health, Career, and Faith*. Harper Collins, 2009.

Kessler, David. *Finding Meaning: the Sixth Stage of Grief*. Scribner, 2019.

Lewis, C. S. *A Grief Observed*. Bantam Books, 1983.

Makoul, Joshua. *Healing Your Wounded Soul: Growing from Pain to Peace*. Chesterton, IN: Ancient Faith Publishing, 2020.

O'Donohue, John. *To Bless the Space between Us: A Book of Blessings*. Harmony Books, 2008.

Rando, Therese A. *Treatment of Complicated Mourning*. Research Press, 1993.

Richardson, Jan L. *The Cure for Sorrow: a Book of Blessings for Times of Grief*. Orlando, FL: Wanton Gospeller Press, 2016.

Rossi, Albert S. *All Is Well*. Chesterton, IN: Ancient Faith Publishing, 2020.

Rotondo, Beth. *Threads of Hope: An Offering for Those Who Grieve*. Weymouth, MA: Stillpoint Press, 2004.

Schroedel, Jenny. *Naming the Child: Hope-Filled Reflections on Miscarriage, Stillbirth, and Infant Death*. Paraclete, 2010.

Schwiebert, Pat, and Chuck DeKlyen. *Tear Soup: A recipe for healing after loss*. Grief Watch, 2005.

Silverman, Phyllis R., Dennis Klass, and Steven L. Nickman, eds. *Continuing Bonds: New understandings of grief*. Taylor & Francis, 1996.

Sittser, Jerry, and Gerald Lawson Sittser. *A Grace Disguised: How the soul grows through loss*. Zondervan, 2004.

Stroebe, Margaret S., Robert O. Hansson, Henk Ed Schut, and Wolfgang Ed Stroebe. *Handbook of bereavement research and practice: Advances in theory and intervention*. American Psychological Association, 2008.

Wolfelt, Alan. *Understanding Your Grief: Ten Essential Touchstones for Finding Hope and Healing Your Heart*. Companion Press, 2004.

Wolterstorff, Nicholas. *Lament for a Son*. Eerdmans, 1987.

Worden, J. William. *Grief Counseling and Grief Therapy: A Handbook for the Mental Health Practitioner*. Springer Publishing Company, 2008.

Endnotes

1   Met. Anthony Bloom, *Beginning to Pray* (Paulist Press, 1970), p. 35.
2   Ibid.
3   Kallistos Ware, *The Inner Kingdom* (Crestwood, NY: St. Vladimir's Seminary Press, 2000), p. 27.
4   Alexander Schmemann, *The Liturgy of Death: Four Previously Unpublished Talks* (Crestwood, NY: St. Vladimir's Seminary Press, 2016), p. 156.
5   John Behr, *The Mystery of Christ: Life in Death* (Yonkers, NY: St. Vladimir's Seminary Press, 2006), p. 33.
6   Ibid., p. 35.
7   St. Gregory of Nyssa, in Behr, p. 38.
8   Ibid.
9   Ibid.
10   Ibid., p. 40.
11   Ibid., p. 99.
12   Ibid.
13   Fr. Thomas Hopko, "The Word of the Cross," Ancient Faith Ministries, February 2011, https://www.ancientfaith.com/specials/hopko_lectures/the_word_of_the_cross_part_1.
14   Ibid.
15   Hopko, "The Word of the Cross."
16   Ibid.
17   Hans Boersma, "'Numbed with Grief': Gregory of Nyssa on Bereavement and Hope," *Journal of Spiritual Formation and Soul Care* 7, no. 1 (2014): p. 58.
18   Boersma, "Numbed with Grief," p. 47.
19   St. Gregory of Nyssa, *On the Soul and the Resurrection* (Crestwood, NY: St. Vladimir's Seminary Press, 1993), in Boersma, p. 48.
20   Boersma, "Numbed with Grief," p. 50.
21   Ibid.
22   Ibid., p. 57.
23   Ibid.
24   Ibid.
25   Schmemann, *Liturgy of Death*, p. 162.

26 Ibid.
27 Alexis Vinogradov, "*Votserkovlenie Zhizni*—The Churching of Life and Culture," *St. Vladimir's Theological Quarterly*, 53 2–3 (2009): p. 344.
28 Alan Wolfelt, "Help and Support when Planning a Funeral," Batesville, www.batesville.com.
29 Ibid.
30 Nicholas Denysenko, "Death and Dying in Orthodox Liturgy," *Religions* 8, no. 2 (2017): p. 25.
31 Ibid.
32 Ibid., p. 2.
33 Ibid.
34 Ibid., p. 3-4.
35 John Breck, "Eucharistic Offering," Orthodox Church in America, accessed November 4, 2019, https://www.oca.org/reflections/Fr. -john-breck/eucharistic-offering.
36 Schmemann, *Liturgy of Death*, pp. 127–128.
37 Ibid.
38 Denysenko, p. 25.
39 Ibid.
40 Ibid., p. 5.
41 Ibid., p. 12.
42 Schmemann, *Liturgy of Death*, p. 49.
43 "Order for the Burial of a Layperson," Orthodox Church in America, 2017. https://www.oca.org/files/PDF/Music/Burial/burial-of-layperson.pdf. Accessed Nov. 11, 2019.
44 Ibid.
45 *AOCA Service Book*, pp. 192–193.
46 Charlie Marge (Sacred Music Coordinator, Diocese of Worcester & New England, Antiochian Archdiocese), conversation with author, November 29, 2019.
47 Charlie Marge, who also noted: "During the Paschal Season (during Bright Week for the Greeks, entire 40 days for the Antiochians), practically the entire funeral service is made up of Paschal hymns. All those Tone 6 hymns are gone because the mindset of the church is so predominantly resurrectional at that time. It's almost like the church acknowledges that it's hard to grieve during that season. I think deep down, many of us hope that our own funerals will happen during this time so that our loved ones can be overwhelmed with the joy and beauty of the Resurrection."
48 Tone 2, Orthodox Burial of the Dead, *AOCA Service Book*, p. 193.
49 Tone 8, Orthodox Burial of the Dead, *AOCA Service Book*, p. 194.
50 Ibid.
51 Mark Barna, "A Christian Ending," Ancient Faith Ministries (podcast), July 2013, https://www.ancientfaith.com/podcasts/christianending

52 *AOCA Service Book*, p. 75.

53 Ibid., p. 81.

54 Ibid.

55 Lamentations of Holy Week, *AOCA Service Book*, Stasis 2.

56 Stasis 1, *AOCA Service Book*.

57 Ibid.

58 Ibid., Stasis 2.

59 Charlie Marge.

60 Ibid.

61 C.S. Lewis, *A Grief Observed* (Bantam Books, 1983), pp. 28–29.

62 Justin Brierly, "3 Reasons Why God Allows Suffering," *Premier Christianity*, November 20, 2018. https://www.premierchristianity.com/Past-Issues/2016/July-2016/3-reasons-why-God-allows-suffering. In conversation with Fr Sergius Halvorsen.

63 *AOCA Service Book*, 185.

64 Sergius Halvorsen, conversation with author, October 24, 2019.

65 Nicholas Solak, conversation with author, October 21, 2019.

66 Solak.

67 Halvorsen.

68 Ibid.

69 St. Gregory of Nyssa, *Funeral Oration on Meletius*, in Boersma, 51.

70 Ibid., 52.

71 St. Gregory of Nyssa, *Oratio consolatoria in Pulcheriam*, in Boersma, 52.

72 St. Gregory of Nyssa, *Oration funebris in Flacillam imperatricem*, in Boersma, 53.

73 Halvorsen.

74 Ibid.

75 Ibid.

76 Ibid.

77 Orthodox Church in America, "Prayers for the Departed," www.oca.org, accessed November 13, 2019.

78 Greek Orthodox Archdioceses of Australia, "Death, Mourning, and Eternal Life," www.greekorthdox.org.au, accessed Nov 7, 2019.

79 M. Therese Lysaught, "Geographies and Accompaniment: Toward an Ecclesial Re-ordering of the Art of Dying," *Studies in Christian Ethics* 29, no. 3 (2016): 286–293.

80 Ibid.

81 *AOCA Service Book*, p. 184.

82 Alan Wolfelt, *Understanding Your Grief: Ten Essential Touchstones for Finding Hope and Healing Your Heart* (Companion Press, 2004), p. 33.

83 M. Katherine Shear, "Getting straight about grief," *Depression and anxiety* 29, no. 6 (2012): p. 461–464.

84 Ibid., p. 461.

85   J. William Worden, *Grief Counseling and Grief Therapy: A Handbook for the Mental Health Practitioner* (Springer Publishing Company, 2008).

86   Margaret S. Stroebe, et.al, *Handbook of bereavement research and practice: Advances in theory and intervention* (American Psychological Association, 2008).

87   What's Your Grief? *Anticipatory Grief: A Guide to Impending Loss.* Published: What's Your Grief? 2015. Print.

88   Lucy Bregman, *Beyond Silence and Denial: Death and Dying Reconsidered* (Westminster John Knox Press, 1999), p. 106.

89   Ibid.

90   See, for example, Doka, K. J. and Tucci, A. S. eds., 2011. *Beyond Kübler-Ross: New perspectives on death, dying and grief.* Washington, DC: Hospice Foundation of America, and Corr, C. A., 2015. Let's stop "staging" persons who are coping with loss. *Illness, Crisis & Loss,* 23(3), pp. 226-241.

91   Worden, *Grief Counseling,* p. 50.

92   Ibid.

93   Therese A. Rando, *Treatment of complicated mourning* (Research Press, 1993).

94   Kenneth J. Doka, *Disenfranchised grief: Recognizing hidden sorrow* (Lexington, MA: Lexington Books, 1989), p. 7.

95   Alan Wolfelt, *The Understanding Your Grief Support Group Guide: Starting and Leading a Bereavement Support Group* (United States: Companion Press, 2004).

96   Ibid.

97   Ibid.

98   Ibid., 3.

99   Ibid., p. xi.

100   Brian Mellonie, *Lifetimes: The Beautiful Way to Explain Death to Children* (Paw Prints, 2009).

101   Alquin Gliane and Cedric Gliane, *The Butterfly Field* (St. Louis: Rock Publishing Company, 2001).

102   Pat Schwiebert, Chuck DeKlyen, and Taylor Bills, *Tear Soup: a Recipe for Healing after Loss* (Portland: Grief Watch, 2018).

103   Patrice Karst and Joanne Lew-Vriethoff, *The Invisible String* (New York: Little, Brown and Company, 2018).

104   Phyllis R. Silverman, Dennis Klass, and Steven L. Nickman, *Continuing bonds: New understandings of grief* (Taylor & Francis, 1996).

105   Silverman, *Continuing Bonds,* p. 477.

106   Elizabeth A. Gassin, and Gregory J. Lengel, "Forgiveness and attachment: a link that survives the grave?" (Journal of Psychology and Theology 39, no. 4, 2011): pp. 316–329.

107   Paschal Homily of St. John Chrysostom.

108   Schmemman, *Liturgy of Death,* p. 188.

109   Anthony M. Coniaris, *Surviving the Loss of a Loved One* (Light and Life Pub.,

2005), p. 242.

110 Schmemann, *Liturgy of Death*, p. 132.

111 Dean Theophilos, conversation with author at the Annual Conference of the Orthodox Christian Association of Medicine, Psychology, and Religion, 2019.

112 Jan Richardson, *The Cure for Sorrow: A Book of Blessings for Times of Grief* (Wanton Gospeller Press, 2016) p. 33.

113 Emily Nagoski and Amelia Nagoski, *Burnout: The Secret to Unlocking the Stress Cycle* (Ballatyne Books, 2019), p. 14.

114 "Service After a Miscarriage or Stillbirth." https://www.oca.org/orthodoxy/prayers/service-after-a-miscarriage-or-stillbirth. Accessed March 8, 2022.

115 John O'Donohue, *To bless the space between us: A book of blessings* (Harmony Books, 2008).

116 "A Prayer for Every Hour," *The Ancient Faith Prayer Book* (Chesterton, IN: Ancient Faith Publishing, 2014), p. 20.

117 Paschal Sermon of St. John Chrysostom, Matins of Pascha.

118 St. Sophrony of Essex, in *St. Silouan the Athonite* (Yonkers, NY: St. Vladimir's Seminary Press, 1999).

119 Sarah Byrne-Martelli, "Service of Remembrance and Hope," Division of Palliative Medicine, Massachusetts General Hospital, 2019.

120 St. Julian of Norwich, in Richard Chilson, *All Will Be Well: Based on the Classic Spirituality of Julian of Norwich* (Notre Dame, IN: Ave Maria Press, 1995).

121 Rainer Maria Rilke, *Letters to a Young Poet* (Mineola, NY: Dover Publications, Inc., 2019).

122 *St. Julian of Norwich: Showings* (New York: Paulist Press, 1978).

123 Nicholas Woltersdorff, *Lament for a Son* (Grand Rapids, MI: Eerdmans, 1987).

124 St. Isaac the Syrian, in Anthony Coniaris, *Surviving the Loss of a Loved One* (Minneapolis, MN: Light and Life Pub., 2005), 101.

125 Henri J. M. Nouwen, *In Sorrow Shared: a Combined Edition of the Nouwen Classics in Memoriam and a Letter of Consolation* (Ave Maria Press, 2011).

126 Elder Porphyrios, *Wounded by Love* (Limni: Denise Harvey Pub., 2003).

127 St. John Chrysostom, in Coniaris, *Surviving the Loss of a Loved One*, 49.

128 Coniaris, *Surviving the Loss of a Loved One*, p. 20.

129 St. Francis de Sales, *A Selection from the Spiritual Letters of St. Francis de Sales* (London: Sidney Lear, 1880).

130 Metropolitan Anthony of Sourozh, in Coniaris, p. 98.

131 Lewis, *A Grief Observed*, p. 21.

132 Ibid.

133 Schmemann, *Liturgy of Death*, pp. 127–128.

134 Ibid.

135 I recommend the Assembly of Bishops' Directory of Mental Health Pro-

viders, https://www.assemblyofbishops.org/directories/mental-health/.
For resources integrating the Orthodox Faith and related topics, including
online video resources, I recommend the Orthodox Christian Association of
Medicine, Psychology, and Religion at https://ocampr.org/. If an Orthodox
therapist in your area is not available, you may search on Psychology Today
and sort by area, faith group, insurance provider, and other topics: https://
www.psychologytoday.com/us/therapists

136 Yalom, Irvin D., and Molyn Leszcz. *The Theory and Practice of Group Psycho-
therapy.* New York: Basic Books, 2005.

S ARAH BYRNE-MARTELLI IS an Orthodox board-certified chaplain and bereavement counselor who has served in acute care, palliative care, and hospice since 2002. In her role as a chaplain, she cares for patients and families who are facing serious illness, grief, and loss. Sarah holds a DMin from St. Vladimir's Orthodox Theological Seminary and an MDiv from Harvard Divinity School. She is on the Board of the Orthodox Christian Association of Medicine, Psychology, and Religion (OCAMPR). Sarah attends St. Mary Orthodox Church in Cambridge, MA, with her husband, Dr. Peter Martelli, and their son, Rafael.

We hope you have enjoyed and benefited from this book. Your financial support makes it possible to continue our non-profit ministry both in print and online. Because the proceeds from our book sales only partially cover the costs of operating **Ancient Faith Publishing** and **Ancient Faith Radio**, we greatly appreciate the generosity of our readers and listeners. Donations are tax deductible and can be made at **www.ancient-faith.com**.

To view our other publications, please visit our website:
store.ancientfaith.com

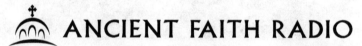 ANCIENT FAITH RADIO

Bringing you Orthodox Christian music, readings, prayers, teaching, and podcasts 24 hours a day since 2004 at
www.ancientfaith.com

CPSIA information can be obtained
at www.ICGtesting.com
Printed in the USA
LVHW041547140523
746958LV00006B/741